Indian Jades

INDIAN JADES

M.L. Nigam

SHARADA

SHARADA PUBLISHING HOUSE

DELHI

First Published 2019

ISBN: 978-93-83221-26-4
₹ 1200

Published by

SHARADA PUBLISHING HOUSE
111, Vidya Vihar Apartment
Sector-9, Rohini, Delhi-110 085 (INDIA)
Ph.: +91-11-4702 6210, 2755 2102
E-mail : bansal_sph@rediffmail.com
books@sharadabooks.com
Website : www.sharadabooks.com

Printed at

Delhi

Contents

Preface

The word 'Jade' known as *L'ejade* in French during the seventeenth century and *Piedra de hijada* in Spanish, first occurs in 1727 in Chamber's Cyclopedia. It includes all the three varieties, viz. Nephrite,[1] Jadeite and Chloromelanite, generally found in the Khotan and Yarkand regions of eastern Turkistan and upper Burma. The Chinese synonym for Jade, 'Yu', which initially covered a wider range of semi-precious stones like the agate, quartz and fluor families, was quarried mainly from the regions of Yarkand, Khotan, Kaskem Valley and the slopes of Kuen-Lun and Nan Shah mountains.[2] In China, true Jade means Nephrite. Jadeite, which was imported through the province of Yunnan in Burma, is known as Yunnan Yu or "Fei-ts'ui". In the dictionary of English, Persian and Arabic by John Richardson, which was printed in 1810 CE the Persian word 'Yashm' has been translated as 'Agate' and not as 'Jade', the use of which probably, had not become so common till that time in the English language. Another dictionary of Persian, Arabic and English by Francis Johnson, printed in 1852, mentions the term *yashb* which stands for 'Jasper', especially a whitish kind of stone found on Mont Imaus. The same dictionary refers to a Persian word 'Yashm' which means a sort of Jasper or Agate. In the language of Mongols, the term 'Khas' stands for Jade, whereas in the Turkish language, the term 'Sootash' is also used in the same sense.[3] The term 'Pa-zahar' of Persian origin, which means antidote to poison, was also probably used for Jade as it is evident from an inscription on a wine cup which was engraved with the name of Emperor Jahangir at Mandu in 1617 CE and is now in the collection of Bharat Kala Bhavan, Varanasi. The reputation of Jade that it worked as an antidote to poison was probably the reason for a large number of wine cups, opium container , bowls and water pots to have been fashioned out of this rare and costly material, both in Persia and India.

It is not known exactly as what made the Chinese develop a blind faith in the supernatural powers and mystic qualities of Jade. The Chinese held Jade in such high esteem that it was considered as a bestower of good health, fortune and divine truth, so much so that it became an essential commodity to be offered on certain occasions, such as the royal coronations and death ceremonies. As a scholar puts it, ' it is curious to note that Chinese carving in Jade developed gradually from the purely mythological type, used in religious ceremonies, to a grotesquely symbolic type, derived from many influences and similar in design to art –forms already existing in other parts of the world, until becoming utilitarian, it finally reached, during the Ch'ien Lung period, a high degree of decorative perfection.[4] It is however, doubtless that the wide range of colours, sonorousness and smooth hard surface with a soft greasy appearance after it is polished, must have prompted the use of Jade in fashioning exquisite objects of art at early stages. It is generally believed that the carvings developed from the early spear heads and weapons to ritual tokens and thence to the Imperial emblems of the Chou dynasty.

Mineralogical Properties

There has been a good deal of confusion regarding the

hardness and basic properties of Jade. This is primarily due to the fact that Jade is subjected to the technique of abrading with the help of certain abrasives specially prepared for the task. In fact, hardness of Nephrite, Jadeite and Chloromeamite are relatively 6½, 6¾ to 7 points which are lesser than those of quartz, topaz, corundum (ruby, etc.) and diamond. Hence, the above minerals act as abrasives in fashioning Jade- objects. The basic mineralogical properties present in all kinds of Jade are silica, alumina and soda in various quantities. In fact, the colour in Jade is due to the presence of small quantities of various chemicals, mainly compounds of iron, manganese and chromium.[5] The Nephrite variety which is composed mainly of silica and manganese, owes its green colour due to the amount of iron present in it. However, pure white Jade, the real 'mutton fat' variety, is also Nephrite. The apple-green and emerald- green colours, that are characteristics of Jadeite, are produced by chromium. Mauve and light blue colours are found in Jadeite only. The black colour of Chloromelanite is due to excessive concentration of an iron compound.

	Nephrite percent	*Jadeite percent*	*Chloromelanite percent*
Silica	58.00	58.24	56.12
Alumina	1.30	24.77	14.96
Magnesia	24.18	0.45	2.79
Soda	1.28	14.70	10.99
Ferrous Oxide	2.07	-	6.54
Ferric Oxide	-	1.01	3.34
Lime	13.24	0.69	5.17
Potash	-	1.55	Trace
Manganese oxide	-	-	0.47
Titanium Dioxide	-	-	0.19
	100.07	101.41	100.57

According to *Mani-Mala*, a treatise on Indian gemology,

the synonym of jade in Sanskrit language is 'pilu' which is mentioned there as one of the up-ratnas or a minor gem. Describing its multiple shades and characteristics, the aforesaid text mentions that jade has many varieties, such as the smoke-coloured, white, green shaded with white and it is also hard, non-transparent and slightly lustrous. It further says that 'pilu' is a very hard variety of stone, possessing different types of colours. In order to quality, the specimens known as "Jeoni" which is hard and transparent as looking glass, is considered to be the best. Next is "subj-mael-zurdi", shaded with green and yellow, then comes "subj-mael-safedi", a mixture of green and white and the last quality is 'kafuri' or pure white like camphor. Whereas Timurid craftsmen preferred dark green nephrite for their works, the Indian artisans of Akbar's period used mostly the white jade for their products. Although the early jade specimens of Jahangir's period are of dark green colour, the artisans of Shah Jahan period again preferred milky white jade for their beautiful jade specimens.

My book, *Jade Collection in the Salar Jung Museum, Hyderabad,* was published in 1979. Since then, the study and researches on Indian Jade-art have advanced considerably. A good number of new discoveries, both archaeological and literary, have been made in the realm of jade-art of India which throws a flood of light on the subject. There are a large number of museums in India and abroad which include enormous wealth of Indian jade specimens in their collections. Barring Salar Jung Museum, which possesses the largest and some of the rarest jade pieces of Indian origin, there are other Indian museums such as the Bharat Kala Bhavan, Varanasi; National Museum, New Delhi; Chhatrapati Shivaji Maharaj Vastu Sangrahalaya, Mumbai; State Museum, Hyderabad, and the State Museum, Lucknow in U.P., which have Indian jades. There is also a private collection housing the Indian jade objects, called the Singhania Collection at Mumbai.

Among the foreign museums and art-galleries, which possess Indian jades are the British museum, London, Victoria & Albert Museum, London, U.K., the Metropolitan Museum of Art, New York; Los Angeles County Museum, Los Angeles; Seattle Art Museum, Washington, U.S.A.; the National Palace Museum, Taipei, Taiwan, the Palace Museum, Peking, China. The Al-Sabah Collection, Kuwait National Museum, Kuwait and Topkapi Palace Museum, Istanbul.

The Salar Jung Museum, Hyderabad, is singularly lucky to possess the largest collection of Indian Jade, including some of the rarest specimens, inscribed and dated, which throw a welcome light to settle the long-standing controversy about the origin of Indian jade-art tradition. There are roughly one thousand jade pieces in the said collection which can be divided into two main categories. Firstly, the food vessels and the second which consists of miscellaneous objects. The food vessels include bowls, cups, plates, scoops, ladels, vases and pots to hold drinks and other eatables. Among the miscellaneous objects, there are jars, flasks, jugs, boxes, pen-cases, lamp-stands, censers, book-stands, mirror frames, gunpowder flasks, huqqa mohnals, sword and dagger handles, Zafar-Takias, back-scratchers, jewellery pendants etc., which were used by the Mughal nobility and royal household.

Although, the Salar Jung Museum, Hyderabad, possesses around thousand Indian jade specimens, no systematic study was made earlier. These jade-objects were earlier considered mostly to be of Chinese origin. Meanwhile, some very interesting and positive discoveries have taken place and which throw a welcome light on this subject.

It is indeed, gratifying to note that the Indian jade-art has now received universal recognition as an independent academic discipline. Several very authentic and trustworthy publications have come out in the form of catalogues, monographs, books and learned research-articles. The new information have been brought out by scholars in different parts of the world. In this regard, the name of Teng-Shu-Ping deserves special mention for bringing out two voluminous catalogues of Indian (Hindustan) jade housed in the National Palace Museum, Taipei. The researches of Teng-Shu-Ping have yielded a lot of very useful information on the brisk jade-trade that was going on between India and China during the reign of the Chinese emperor, Ch'ien-lung (1758-1795). The other important scholar, James C.Y. Watt has published a catalogue of the jade collection in the Seattle Art Museum which includes both the Chinese and Indian jade-specimens. He has given the title "Mughal and Mughal-Style jades" for Indian jade. Similarly, Manual Keene, along with Salam Kaouksi, have brought out an illustrated catalogue, Treasury of the World-Jwelled Arts of India in the age of the mughals. Robert Skelton is, no doubt, one of the pioneers who brought international recognition to the art of Indian jade-carving. Yet other scholar, Stephen Markel, has also contributed a number of research papers to highlight the Indian jade collection in the Los Angeles County Museum, Los Angeles.

In this regard, our in-depth study and continued research-work on the Indian Jade Collection in Salar Jung Museum has yielded very fruitful results which would dispel all existing confusion and controversies about the origin and development of Indian jade-art. A number of new discoveries, both archaeological and literary, which are of great consequence and value, have been made during our prolonged study of the subject. Our researches are hence wide-based, covering the Central Asian, Chinese, Persian and Indian sources.

So far as the problem of the availability of jade in India is concerned, the western scholars believed that Indians did not know about jade stone as raw-material till the age of Akbar, as good quality of jade is not found in India. In this regard, it would be quite interesting to know that India, right from the beginning of the Christian era, had very close and cardial relationship with the jade producing centers of sinkiang region in Central Asia. In fact, Khotan, where the best variety of nephrite jade is found, was inhabited by the Hindu and Buddhist missionaries who had gone there from India to propagate their respective faiths sometime during 1st-2nd century CE. The variety of archaeological discoveries from khotan and its vicinity made by Sir M. Aurel Stein and others have provided enough evidence to suggest that people residing there in the past were Indians, following Buddhism as their religion. Their spoken language was archaic Sanskrit and their written characters (as well as their laws and literature) resemble the Indian model. It is, therefore, quite obvious that Indians relationship with Khotan was very intimate and the frequent movement of people from India to Central Asia and vice-versa must have made Indians aware of jade which was a very precious commodity for export to other countries.

Further, the Chinese traveler, Hiuen-T'sang, who visited India during seventh century, CE, does mention in his travel accounts that jade, was a commodity of regular commercial transaction between India and Central Asia. Hence, to presume that the Indians did not have the knowledge of jade till seventeenth century CE is quite unconvincing. Hiuen-T'sang was a great Chinese scholar and his statement about jade as a commodity of regular transaction between India and Central Asia cannot be doubted. So far technology is concerned; it was Robert Skelton who declared that Indians had the knowledge of carving of hard stones, such as crystal even during first and second century CE. A number of crystal reliquaries have been excavated from the Buddhist stupas belonging to early centuries of the Christian Era. He cited an example of a crystal reliquary which is carved in the form of a goose and presently kept in the British Museum, London. As crystal is harder then jade, Indian stone-carvers could not have found it difficult to carve jade for making their beautiful specimens. We may thus conclude that Indians had knowledge of jade as a raw material and also the knowledge of hard stone technology to carve objects of harder material than jade during 2nd-1st century BCE, if not earlier.

Agastya-Samhita

As regards to the tools and technology, the fateful discovery of Agastya-samhita, a Sanskrit manuscript on gemology which was copied from an earlier text in 1334 CE, provides very valuable information regarding the highly developed tools and technology which India possessed during fourteenth century CE. The variety of tools which were made by employing indigenous materials and used for different specific purposes are described there in great details. For example, nine varieties of Grinding Wheels and six types of Diamond drills are mentioned for sawing or slicing, for boring holes, for carving out figures for engraving, for trimming the edges, for removing impurities of the stones and for polishing. It leaves no room for doubt that Indian artisans working on precious and semi-precious hard stones were fully aware and equipped with the highly advanced hard-stone technology to deal with all types of jade works with great skill and perfection during fourteenth century CE. It further mentions the names of various materials used and so also the methods to make their tools. It is thus evident that India had developed a fully accomplished technology and tools to deal with hard stones, like jade. This view is further confirmed by a number of discoveries which can be dated to pre-Mughal era.

The present treatise "Indian Jades" is divided into three chapters. The first chapter deals with the various Indian, Persian and Chinese sources which are found useful to know the history of Indian jade carving tradition. The earlier views of the western scholars, like Hansford, who believed that all Indian jades were carved by the Chinese, have been discussed in detail so as to clear the various doubts which existed during the early stages of this study. It has been now proved beyond doubt that India did import jade as the raw material from the Central Asian regions like Khotan, Yarkand and Kashgarh. Thus, there was a regular socio-religious contact between India and Central Asia via Tibet. The Indian carvan merchants, who were trading with the China through Central Asia, brought jade and other precious material from China. As we have stated earlier, the Chinese traveller, Hieun-T'sang, has very clearly mentioned that jade was a commodity of regular transaction between India and China. As far as the tools and technology is concerned, the various archaeological and literary sources have been fully discussed to prove that India had developed the full-fledge technology and tools to carve hard stones like crystal, agate etc., which are harder than jade. The fateful discovery of a Sanskrit manuscript *Agastya Samhita* belonging to fourteenth century CE provides very useful information about the various types of tools which could easily carve even the precious stones like rubies, emerald and diamond etc. Thus, a fully accomplished hard-stone technology to carve jade was developed in India even during pre-Christian period

The Chinese Sources

There are a good number of references pertaining to the art of Indian jade carving which occur in some of the early royal records of China. The earliest mention of Indian jade, datable to 2nd-1st century BCE, is found in the royal records of the Han (six dynasties) period where it is stated that the people of shen-tu (sindh) had sent tribute gift of a bridal made of interlocking rings of white jade to the Han emperor, Wu-ti (140-87 BCE). The Liang-shu or the History of the Liang dynasty (502-557 CE) also records that a ruler of the Gupta dynasty of north India sent a jade "Liu-Li (spittoon) as a gift during the Tien-Chien reign period (557 CE). It has thus rightly been observed" that the early references quoted above nonetheless raise the possibility that nephrite jade was itself one of the materials used by the hard-stone carvers of northern India between the second century BCE and sixth century CE.

Persian Manuscript — *Khawasul Jawahar*

Yet, another very important discovery made in this regard is that of a Persian manuscript, *Khawasul Jawahar* which is presently housed in the library of Salar Jung Museum, Hyderabad. It throws a very important information on the history of jade-carving tradition in Central Asia. It says that the first Timurid ruler who introduced the art of jade carving in Central Asia was Shah Rukh who was a great patron of art and learning. Prior to the reign of Shah Rukh, the Turks of Mawarunhar and Khorasan did not take interest in the art of jade-carving. It was, however from the period of Shah Rukh that the turks got interested in it and later they not only learnt this art but also got mastery over it. The Turks learnt this art from the kafirs who were known for the mastery over this art. Who were these kafirs? Who taught this art to Turks? This question has been discussed in great detail in the present Treatise.

The second chapter is devoted to a vary analytical study of all the important Mughal jades which were carved under the Mughal emperors. There existed a controversy about the jade carving during Aurangzeb time. Some scholars believed that Indian arts like dance, music and paintings etc., suffered a setback during Aurangzeb period because of the strong orthodox nature of Aurangzeb. Besides, the economic condition of the north Indian regions had dwindled and hence, there was a lack of proper patronage to all arts and crafts. This view however, does not seem to be correct because Indian miniature painting continued to flourish during the time of Aurangzeb and even after. So also was the case with the art of jade carving. According to Mohammed Kazim, the court historian of Aurangzeb, the emperor had discarded gold and opted for jade for making his personal jewellery. This must have boosted the jade trade as the courtiers must have also followed the emperor for using jade for their personal jewellery and other domestic purposes.

Discovery of an Archaic Jade book-stand

Further, an archaeological discovery of a Jade Quran-stand (Rehl) (no. 14/XLIX) in the collection of Salar Jung Museum, Hyderabad, is of paramount interest to us, as it throws fresh light on the history of Indian jade-carving. It bears inscriptions on either side in archaic characters, which are dated in "Sam 607 Hijra" (1209-10 CE) and mentions the name of its owner, Shamsuddin Altamish Padshah. It is thus, the earliest of the so-called Islamic jades of Indian origin known so far anywhere in the world. The king, Shams-ud-din Altamish was the ruler of the slave dynasty of Indian history who ascended the throne of Delhi in India in 1209-10 CE. It shows that the art of jade-carving was very well known in India much earlier to the advent of the Mughals.

The third chapter, "Jade under later Mughals and the jade-trade with China via Sinkiang" throws light on the history of Indian jade-carving which continued till the first quarter of ninteenth century CE. A good deal of information regarding the Indian jade trade with the Eastern World is known from the verses composed by the Chinese ruler, Ch'ien-lung which he wrote in praise of Indian jade-objects. He wrote verses on the jade specimens which were presented to him. Some of the verses are also found inscribed on the surface of the jade objects. It was a long period from 1756-1795 that the Chinese ruler went on writing such verse which throw a very authentic and trustworthy account of the jade trade between India and China. Further, the verses also throw a very interesting and eye-witness account of the evolutionary changes in Indian jade carving which went on taking place during this period. He uses metaphors and similes to appreciate the beauty and technical skill of Indian jade artist. In fact, the artists of Aurangzeb in the initial stages followed the technique and decorative motifs and designs which were prevalent during Shah Jahan period. However, the artisans made several changes by adopting Chinese technique in their art so as to make it more acceptable to the Chinese clientel. Further, the thinness of carving increased so as to please the Chinese emperor. Yet another important source which throws light on the subject is the travel account of Francis Bernier who remained in India during the reign of Shah Jahan and Aurangzeb.

The purpose of this treatise is to share our thoughts and researches with other scholars and researchers to reach an understanding in view of the recent discoveries and researches about the origin and development of the Indian jade-art. No doubt, a good deal of work has been done in this regard all over the world yet, much remains still to be done to come to a satisfactory conclusion. Many scholars still believe that the art of Indian jade-carving came into existence after the advent of Mughals in India during seventeenth century CE.

It is still believed that Indians came to know of jade stone during the rule of Mughals in India. Thus there still exists a good deal of confusion and controversy about the origin and development of Indian jade art. Where does the problem lie?

In fact, most of the studies on this subject, which have appeared so far, are object-oriented. Scant attention has been paid to contemporary literary works, such as manuscripts, historical records and travelogues which contain enormous information to supplement and strengthen our study. Unless we study and assimilate such literary data, our studies will remain incomplete. It is high time that we remove this lacunae and try to present a correct and coherent picture of Indian jade-art.

I hope, our present treatise will prove to be a positive step in this direction.

M.L. Nigam

Acknowledgements

I must express my deep sense of gratitude to all such scholars whose works and researches have been useful to me to complete this work. I am equally grateful to all such authorities of various institutions such as British Museum, London; Victoria and Albert Museum, London; Metropolitan Museum of Art, New York; Salar Jung Museum, Hyderabad; Chhatrapati Shivaji Maharaj Vastu Sangrahalaya, Mumbai; National Museum, New Delhi and Bharat Kala Bhavan, Varanasi whose transparencies and photographs to illustrate in my present book. I must also thank Dr Rahmat Ali Khan, who studied and interpreted Persian inscriptions for me which are found inscribed on some jade-objects.

I am grateful to all my family members, particularly two sons, Sri Pradeep Nigam and Sri Anup Nigam and my daughter Dr Anupama Bhatnagar and daughter-in-laws, Dr Hema Nigam and Mrs. Shikha Nigam who provided me all help and co-operation in bringing out this book. Last but not least, I must express my sincere thanks to the Sharada Publishing House, who have taken enough pains to bring this book out nicely.

M.L. Nigam

List of Illustrations

Chapter 1

INDIAN JADES – ORIGIN AND DEVELOPMENT

The study of the art of jade-carving in India is a recent phenomenon. Whereas the history of jade-carving in China, which goes back roughly to four thousand years, has been studied and documented in great detail by scholars. The Indian jade-art remained totally unidentified and obscure till 1964 when it was first discussed by the western scholars. It was in 1964 that an exhibition of jade objects brought from different Asian countries such as Central Asia, Ottoman Turkey, Persia and India was organized in London. The scholars who met there made a serious beginning of the subject. However for want of a better name, they called these jades as "Islamic Jades".

We do not agree with the above hypothesis. Firstly, we find no similarity in color form and technique between the Central Asian jades and the early Indian jades which are attributed to Akbar. The Central Asian and Ottoman Turks preferred dark green nephrite for their jade products whereas most of the early jades of Akbar's period are made of white nephrite. The form and technique of the early Central Asian jades are nearer to the Chinese traditions. Secondly, we do not believe that Indians learned the art of jade carving from early Asian and Ottoman Turks. So far the Persians are concerned; they did not take much interest in the art of jade carving. We shall be discussing this problem shortly in great detail.

Some of the Persian motifs and technical devices which occur in early Jahangiri Jades had already appeared in India during the rule of Tughlags and Lodis. So the Indians had already become familiar with such Persian decorative motifs and technical devices and they could reproduce them as and when it was needed. Hence there is no need to call "Indian Jades" as "Islamic" Jades.

The scholars, like John Irwin and Robert Skelton, however made further headway and have contributed a lot towards the systematic study of Indian jade-workmanship. Both the above scholars, however, based their study on two conclusive points. First, India had no knowledge of jade and hence, all Indian jades were produced after the advent of the Mughals in India and secondly, all early Jahangiri jades were inspired by Persian jade-carvers.[2] Thus, there has been a good deal of controversy about the origin of the art of jade-carving in India. The opinion of scholars is divided on this issue. A group of early European scholars believed that all finished objects of jade, bearing even the traditional Indian motifs and designs and sometimes even the names of Indian rulers, were made by the Chinese craftsmen for their Indian customers.[3] Such a negative opinion was based mainly on three grounds. Firstly, good quality of jade is not found in the Indian subcontinent. Secondly, the jade-craft is not found mentioned in the state chronicles of Akbar. Thirdly, some of the jade objects inscribed with the names of Indian rulers in Persian characters, exhibit occasionally an unmistakable similarity with the Chinese mode of carving.

All the above points can easily be explained on the basis of literary and archaeological evidence. Firstly, it is not correct to presume that jade as stone remained unknown till the advent of Mughals in India. Of course, good quality of jade is not found in India yet, Indian Buddhist and Hindu missionaries had reached to the jade producing regions in Central Asia as early as first century CE, if not earlier. There was regular import of jade from Central Asia to India. Indian caravan merchants used to go to China via Tibet to sell Indian merchandise there and in return, bring back Chinese specialties to India which earned a good profit. The Chinese traveller Hiuen-T'sang, who came to India during 7th via Central Asia, informs us that jade was a commodity of regular commercial transaction between India and China during seventh century CE.[4]

Secondly, it is not necessary that everything should find mention in the chronicles written during Akbar's period. The French traveller Bernier, who came to India and remained in Delhi during the reign periods of Shah Jahan and Aurangzeb, speaks very eloquently about the flourishing of Indian jade-art in Delhi and other parts of India. It was Prof. Hansford who first attributed all Indian jade specimens to Chinese workmanship. Writing on this subject in1968, Prof. Hansford concluded by saying, "Indian artists and craftsmen could possibly have equalled or surpassed the Chinese in this characteristically Chinese and highly specialized art and craft in the seventeenth century seems beyond the bounds of probability and, I venture to suggest, of possibility".[5] A year later, the learned professor appears to have revised his opinion by providing an alternative suggestion that Chinese jade carvers were invited by the Mughal court to India where they worked themselves and perhaps eventually trained skillful Indian pupils. Yet, he did not produce any positive evidence to support his hypothesis. Prof. Hansford was probably unaware of the crystal reliquaries datable to the beginning of Christian Era which were found from the excavations of several Buddhist stupas in India.

So far as hard stone technology is concerned. It was Robert Skelton who mentioned that rock crystal was a favourite material in India for making Buddhist relic caskets, Hindu *lingas* and Jain images at least two thousand years ago. He cited an example of an Indian crystal reliquary shaped like a goose in the British Museum, London, which is datable to the beginning of the Christian Era.[6] As crystal is harder than jade, it could not have been difficult for Indian craftsmen to carve jade and produce beautiful jade-objects during Early Medieval Era of Indian history. It is thus beyond doubt that Indians possessed fully accomplished hard stone technology before the advent of the Mughals in India.

Tools and Equipments

Ancient Sanskrit texts make a mention of various types of tools and equipments used for the Indian lapidary. The great poet Kalidas (fifth century CE) speaks of the diamond drills for boring holes into gem-beads. Bhartrahari speaks about the Grinding Wheel (*shana*) for cutting and polishing gems so as to bring luster on them. Yet another text, *Agastya Samhita*, a manual on gemology provides very valuable and detailed information about the various tools and equipments which were employed to cut and polish gems during early mediaeval era of Indian history.[7] It was copied in Nepalika *Samvat* 456 (1334-35 CE) from a manuscript by a Maharashtrian Pandit Damodara at the instance of Prince Rauta Jivasimhadeva during the reign of Maharauta Jaitasimhadeva. It contains elaborate discussion on the tools and equipments of the lapidary. It further deals with various types of materials used and so also the methods to make these tools and equipments. It also informs about the functioning of each tool and equipment as mentioned below.

Grinding Wheels

1. *Kharas:* It was cast with coarse grains of corundum mixed with small quantity of shellac required to bind the corundum grains of the disc together.
2. *Baddhasana*: Its function is not clearly mentioned. It is probably used to smoothen the grains.
3. *Kinasana:* It is supposed to remove the granular parts (*kina*) from the surface of the gem.
4. *Sprstasana*: It is used for making the gem-surface smooth.
5. *Malasana:* It is remover of impurities (*mala*) on the surface of the gem.

The aforesaid varieties were cast with varying proportions of shellac (*laksha*) and corundum (*kuruvinda*). Crushed corundum is thoroughly mixed with molten shellac; the mixture is cooled and moulded into the shape of discs. Apart from these grinding wheels, the text describes one more apparatus for grinding, called *dronika*. This is a wooden mortar, whose inner surface is coated with a layer of mud to which corundum powder is applied. Gems were ground in this apparatus and the depression of the mortar is well noted for cutting gems *encabochon*.

Polishing Wheels

Agastya Samhita has further mentioned four types of polishing wheels, each wheel meant for a separate variety of gems.

1. *Kasthsana*: It is made of smooth Salmali wood (*Salmalia Malabarica* Scott. et Enat.). They applied water while polishing in this wheel.
2. *Mrcchana*: This is cast with equal parts of shellac and

black earth. Besides, ashes of certain trees are also applied to this wheel.

3. *Tamrasana*: This is a copper wheel coated with burnt *gara* (dust of gemstones). This was used for polishing hard gems like the rubies.
4. *Diptisana*: This is made from the timber of *Ravikastha* (*Calotropis gigantea* R.Br.). It was moistened and coated with the ashes of cow-dung. It was used for cabochon cut.

Different types of polishing powders were in vogue to polish the finished precious and semi-precious stones. They were mixed with water and made into paste (*vartika*) and applied to these wheels. The harder and more precious stones (*maharatna*) such as the diamond, ruby, sapphire, emerald, etc. were polished on the copper wheel.

Diamond Drills

Besides, the artisans also used different types of Diamond drills for cutting the edges, carving and engraving of the hard variety of gems. In all, six types of Diamond drills are described in *Agastya Samhita* for different works. The diamond is also known as *vajra* in Sanskrit.

1. *Vajrachakra*: It was used for arranging the gems as per required design. It might have also been used for sawing or polishing the gem stones.
2. *Vedhavajra*: It was used for boring holes in gem beads. Such a diamond drills have been described by Kalidas (fifth century CE)
3. *Sucivajra*: It had a needle sharp tip attached to the drill for carving various designs on the surface of the gem stone.
4. *Lekhavajra*: It was employed for engraving.

5. *Chedanavajra*: It was used for making holes.
6. *Upamarajanavajra*: It was used possibly for removing impurities from the surface of the gem stone.

All the drills were, no doubt, rotated by means of bow. Prof. Irfan Habib has identified one such drill in one of the Indian miniature painting of Mughal Era.[8]

Now coming to the Mughal period, a number of foreign travellers, viz. John Fryer, Thevenot and Tavernier, who visited India during seventeenth century, have left eye-witness accounts on the subject. John Fryer had visited Surat in 1675 where he saw such grinding wheels cast with a mixture of shellac and corundum for cutting and polishing hard gems.[9] He reports, "I went the same day to a Moorman that cuts all sorts of stones, except diamonds, with a certain wheel made of lacquer and stone, ground and incorporated, only to have at Cochin and there the name is not known". It specifically mentions that corundum was available at Cochin only. It was mixed in Salem and Coimbatore districts of Tamil Nadu and was exported by sea to Surat in seventeenth century CE; John Fryer did not know the name of the stone. It was, however, Thevenot who visited Indian mines of Golconda Kingdom in 1666 and described it as white emery. It was called Corind in Telugu.

The foregoing discussion would leave, no doubt, that India had developed full-fledged technology and tools of various kinds to fashion exquisite specimens of the semi-precious and precious stones since third century BCE, if not earlier. The well-known treatise *Arthashastra*, datable to 300 BCE, mentions about the flourishing industry of jewel-making in south India. Thus, the foregoing discussion would suggest that India had developed fully accomplished hard-stone technology right from 2nd-1st century BCE, if not earlier. Hence, India did not require any help or training from the Turkish, Persian or Chinese artisans to carve and make exquisite jade-objects.

Once we admit that jade was a commodity of regular commercial transaction between India and China during seventh century CE, as mentioned by the Chinese traveller, Hiuen-T'sang, and so also that India had developed highly sophisticated hard-stone technology, there should have been no difficulty in making jade-objects, prior to Jahangir's reign period. Let us now examine some literary and archaeological sources, both from India and abroad to know more about the history of Indian jade-carving tradition.

The Chinese Sources

There are a good number of references pertaining to the art of Indian jade-carving which occur in some of the early royal records of China. The earliest mention of Indian jade, datable to 2nd-1st century BCE, is found in the records of the Han (six dynasties) period wherein it is stated that the people of Shen-tu (Sindh) had sent tribute gift of a bridle made of interlocking rings of white jade to the Han emperor Wu-ti (140-87 BCE). The Liang-shu, the History of the Liang dynasty (502-557 CE) also records that a ruler of the Gupta dynasty of north India sent a jade "Liu-Li (spittoon) as a gift during the Tien-Chien reign period (502-557 CE). It has thus been rightly observed by Teng-shu-ping "The early references quoted above nonetheless raise the possibility that nephrite jade was itself one of the materials used by the artisans of northern India between the 2nd century BCE and 6th century A.D." Here, the reference to the jade bridle made of interlocking technique is of special significance. It clearly shows that the Indian lapidaries of 2nd-1st century BCE, were capable of producing such intricate carving in jade with interlocking rings which in subsequent periods become the characteristic feature of Chinese jade workmanship.

Further, the Buddhist missionaries from India, who had gone and settled at Khotan in Central Asia with a view to introduce Buddhism in Far-Eastern country, viz. China, often used to send embassies with precious gifts to the Chinese court. In the records of the Liang dynasty (sixth century CE), it is mentioned that one of the Buddhist rulers of Khotan had sent an embassy to the Chinese ruler along with several costly presents and one such present was a jade statue of the Buddha "carved in foreign lands".[10] It will not be out of context to mention here that a Gupta monarch of north India had sent a jade spittoon to the Chinese court during the same period. Hence, the jade statue of the Buddha which is said to have been carved in "Foreign land" should have been made in India as no other country had the technology of jade-carving, except India at that time.

It will not be out of place to mention here that both the Chinese and Tibetan accounts mention that the foundation of Khotan was laid by the son and ministers of Ashoka, the Mauryan emperor, during the third century BCE.[11] The Chinese came in contact with Khotan only after the conquest of the Tarim basin by Han Wu-ti (140-87 BCE). Prior to that period, Khotan was inhabited by the Hindu and Buddhist missionaries of India who had gone there to propagate their respective religions. A large number of Buddhist monasteries and a rich literature arose in Khotanese language. Khotan was also a repository of Sanskrit texts. A short version of *Ramayana* has also been found in Khotanese. Thus, there existed very close ties between India and Khotan in its early stages.[12]

The Buddhist missionaries, who had gone from India, must have taken along with them the technique of carving of the hard-stones, particularly jade, to Khotan in Central Asia. Otherwise, there is nothing to prove that the original inhabitants of Central Asia possessed the technique of jade-carving during sixth century CE. Thus, the carving of a jade statue of the Buddha during sixth century CE should refer to India alone where Buddhism was then flourishing in its full glory.

The carving of the images of the divinities of the Buddhist pantheon during seventh century CE, in Central Asian regions had become a common phenomenon. The Chinese traveller, Hiuen-T'sang, who had reached India via Central Asian regions during seventh century CE, makes a mention of a big sea-shell shaped jade slab carved with the footprints of the Buddha and kept in the monastery of Kiu-Chi (Kushe) as an object of worship.[13] There is no doubt that the above reference by the Chinese traveller Hiuen-T'sang clearly speaks about a carved pale white jade slab, measuring about 2 feet in length and one foot and eight inches in width, depicting the feet of the Buddha (*Buddhapadas*) which he himself had seen. Hence, there should be no room for doubt that the Buddhist missionaries who had gone and settled in Sinkiang region during the early centuries of the Christian Era had introduced the technique of jade-carving there. They not only established the Buddhist monasteries in the region but also produced the imagery of the Buddhist pantheon for the regular worship of the clergy.

The worship of the feet of the Buddha (*Buddhapadas*) had become popular in India at the time of the Mauryan emperor, Ashoka during third century BCE.[14] A number of stone slabs carved with the feet of the Buddha have been found from Amaravati in Andhra Pradesh (India), belonging to the early phase of the Buddhist art which can be dated to 2nd-1st century BCE. The presence of the *Buddhapadas* carved in a jade slab and kept in the monastery at Kushe would further suggest close contacts and regular movement of the Buddhist clergy from India to Sinkiang region and vice-versa.

Central Asian Evidence

Another very important literary evidence which throws light on the art of jade-carving in Central Asia comes from a Persian manuscript, *Khawasul Jawahara* dealing with the medicinal qualities of precious and semi-precious stones.[15] It is presently housed in the library of the Salar Jung Museum, Hyderabad. The scribe of the manuscript, Mirza Lutf Ali Baig, informs us that it was copied from an earlier treatise on the subject which was originally written by Mohammad Haji under the instructions of the Central Asian monarch, Shah Rukh, a great patron of learning and art. Mirza Lutf Ali Baig copied the same during the reign of Shah Rukh Khan.[16] The period of Shah Rukh can be placed in first quarter of fifteenth century CE. It mentions that the jade was held in high esteem by the nobles of Khata. Their sword-hilts were generally made of jade which was found in seven colors around Kashgar and Khata. However, it was Kafirs living there who had mastery over this art and their workmanship, both in engraving (Naqs-i-Khatai) and in carving out beautiful motifs, forms and figures (Suratgiri), was of such a high standard that the people got puzzled after witnessing the same. It was prized very high and so much so that a jade sword hilt (or belt) was sold in Khata for 5000 gold mohurs. The Kafirs themselves, both men and women, took pride in possessing jade-objects to maintain their social status. Even the tradesmen, who came to Khata, gained importance by acquiring beautiful jade-objects.[17]

The author further informs that the Turks of Mawarunhar and Khorasan initially did not take much interest in the art. It was, however, from the reign period of Shah Rukh, who himself collected jades, that the Turks got interested in this art and later on they not only learnt it but also became experts and produced a good number of master craftsmen in the art of jade-carving. Gauharashad Begum, the wife of Shah Rukh, got prepared a *Pusht* (back of throne?) for her son, Baisanqar Mirza, by spending a large sum of money.[18]

The foregoing remarks, based on an earlier treatise written for the Timurid ruler, Shah Rukh, are of special interest to us to know the history of jade-carving in Central Asia which was initially known and practiced by the Kafirs living at Khata. Secondly, the first Central Asian Timurid ruler who took interest in the art of jade-carving was Shah Rukh. Thirdly, the Turks of the Central Asian regions learnt this art from the Kafirs sometime during 1400 CE, and gained mastery over it. Fortunately for us, the information contained in the Persian treaties, *Khawasul Jawahara* is confirmed by archaeological evidence also. A number of jade specimens belonging to Ulugh Beg, son of Shah Rukh and another scion of the family, 'Ala al-daula, nephew of Ulugh Beg, are known to us. However, not a single example of Timurid jade, which can be dated to pre-Ulugh Beg's Era, has come to our notice. It further strengthens the evidence brought out by *Khawasul Jawahara* that the Turks of Central Asia learnt this art during the period of Shah Rukh Khan, father of Ulugh Beg. The story of Ulugh Beg's capture of two large blocks of jade during his Mughalistan campaign in 1425 CE is already known to us and one of these jade blocks is now placed on the tomb of Timur, the grandfather of Ulugh Beg. No jade specimen, who can be ascribed to a date earlier than that of Ulugh Beg, has come to light so far from Central Asian region. It goes to confirm the statement found mentioned in *Khawasul Jawahara* that the Turks of Mawaraunhar and Khorasan did not know the art of jade-carving prior to the reign of Shah Rukh.

The next problem is that of the identity of the Kafirs who had introduced the art of jade-carving in Central Asia and who transmitted this knowledge to the Turks of Mawaraunhar and Khorasan. In the Islamic context, people other than those who believe in Allah are generally called Kafirs. The travel accounts of Chinese travellers, viz. Fahein and Hiuen-T'sang would testify that the entire Tarim basin had Buddhism as its flourishing religion during 6th-7th centuries CE. Regarding the inhabitants, there it is mentioned, "Their appearance is full of urbanity, and their customs are well regulated (They have Chronicles). Their written characters (as well as their laws and literature) resemble the Indian model; the forms have been somewhat modified; the differences, however, are slight. Their spoken language differs from that of other territories in Central Asia. The law of Buddha is held in great esteem". Besides, the manuscripts found at Dandan-Uiliq and other sites, either of Sanskrit or indigenous texts, also demonstrate the correctness of what the Chinese pilgrim, Hiuen-T'sang had said. Hence, there is no doubt that the Indian Buddhist missionaries were living in large numbers in Tarim basin during seventh century CE. They followed Buddhism and worshipped Buddha.

Islam appears to have entered the Sinkiang region around 1000 CE. It was the beginning of an end of the early ethos of Indian Buddhist culture. The entire region was Islamised. The conversion of the Uighur ruler of Kashgar to Islam marked the death knell of the prevailing religion, Buddhism. The Turkish rulers of Kashgar conquered Khotan in 1106 CE. The other powerful clan in the Sinkiang region, Dzungars, who had escaped conversion, continued to follow Buddhism till late eighteenth century CE, when they were defeated by the army of Ch'ien-lung in 1756-58 CE.

The earliest jade specimens found from the Sinkiang region are the family heirlooms of Uighurs and Dzungars who worshipped Buddhism. When the Ching armies defeated the Dzungars in 1756 and finally in 1758, the Uighurs sent three jade cups at different intervals in 1756, 1758 and 1759 to the Chinese emperor as tribute gifts for their protection from Dzungars. Similarly, the armies of Ch'ien-lung found three large jade plates which were left by the Dzungars at the time of their retreat from the region. The Chinese emperor, while writing a verse to commemorate the event, added that one of these large jade plates was an "Important piece" for the Dzungars that had been passed down through the generations.[19] It would suggest that the large jade plate in question must have been made a couple of centuries earlier either in India or in Khotan itself by the early ancestors of Dzungars, who worshipped Buddhism.

As the heirs of early Buddhist missionaries possessed the technique of jade-carving, they continued to practice the same in the region during the reign period of Shah Rukh also. However, they were known as 'Kafirs' because they had not accepted Islam as their religion. It is thus evident that the Kafirs, as found mentioned in *Khawasul Jawahara*, were no other people than the heirs of the early Indian Buddhist missionaries who had gone from India and settled in Tarim basin. Hence, it will not be inappropriate to suggest that the technique of jade-carving in Central Asia was taken from India by the Buddhist missionaries during the early centuries of the Christian Era. Later, it was learnt by the Turks who gained mastery over this art.

Discovery of an Archaic Jade Book-Stand (1209-10 CE)

Yet another evidence which proves that the art of jade-carving had already come in to vogue in India earlier to the advent of the Mughals is further confirmed by the discovery of a jade book-stand, presently housed in the Salar Jung Museum, Hyderabad (India)[20]. The book-stand (no. 14/XLIX) throws a welcome light on the history of Indian jade-carving. It is an earliest Indian jade so far known in the world. It bears inscriptions on both the sides in archaic characters. On the obverse, it reads, "Shams-ud-din Altamash Padshah", whereas the Reverse reads, "Sam 607 H." amidst a Tree of Life" motif. It measures H. 15.6 cm and W. 10 cm. The book-stand is made out of a single block of white jade. It is carved in conical-shaped arch of early Sultanate architecture. The upper rim of the stand is carved with ridges to the highest point at the centre and then presenting slopes on two side directions. The outside surface is decked with floral motif executed in low relief. The 'Tree of life' motif springs out of a small vase and ends with a full blown, eight-petalled flower at the top with side branches and leaves spreading around.

In order to know the genuineness of the inscription and the date of the jade book-stand, we approached Robert Skeleton, a well-known authority on this subject, for help. He raised following points which should be answered to establish the genuineness of the aforesaid book stand.

Firstly, the script of the legend, as Robert Skelton believed, is not the same which we find in the other inscribed architectural panels of the period of Altamash. Secondly, the name of the owner of the *Quran* stand is inscribed here as Altamash and not Iltutamish. Skelton believed that the form 'Altamash' is the later rendering of the original name given by Badauni at much later date. Thirdly, the rulers of the early Sultanate period are generally mentioned in their records as 'Sultan' and not "Padshah". The date and the authenticity of *Quran* stand could be established beyond all doubts provided the above questions are settled satisfactorily.

In this regard, a careful scrutiny of the legends inscribed on coins, architectural panels and other contemporary records of the reign of the said ruler would probably meet the above objections. So far the script of our inscription is concerned, it is engraved with archaic characters which neither represent the Naskh script found in earlier inscriptions of the period of Altamash, nor it is a developed form of Nastaliq of early Mughal Era. For example, the curves in the lettering are not the same parallel curves as are found in the regular Nastaliq script. Similarly, the dots in Nastaliq script should be square whereas they are circular in the present inscription. In fact, the characters represent the initial stages of Nastaliq script while it was in the process of evolution.

The theory that the form 'Altamash' is a later rendering of the original name of Iltutamish, does not seem to be true as both the forms are found inscribed on the coins issued during lifetime of the slave king. Similarly, the word '*Padshah*' also occurs in a fragmentary inscription from Aligarh which belongs to the period of Altamash wherein he has been mentioned as the king of Islam (*padshah*).

The owner of the book-stand, as per the inscriptions on both sides, was Altamash, a king of the slave dynasty. It is known that Shams-ud-din Altamash ascended the throne of Delhi in 607H (1209-10 CE). The jade book-stand in the Salar Jung Museum, therefore, can easily be attributed to the slave King, Altamash who ruled at the beginning of thirteenth century CE, He was famous for his religious temperament and leanings towards Islam. During this period, the art of calligraphy had reached its highest excellence and many pocket size editions of the Holy *Quran* were written by Turks and Persians in Naskh characters. It is, therefore, logical to believe that this unique rare art-object of sacred nature might have been fashioned as a gift for the new ruler, Shams-ud-din Altamash, who ascended the throne of Delhi in 607 H., equivalent to 1209-10 CE.

It must also be pointed here that the Sultan Shams-ud-din Altamash, who ascended the throne of Delhi in 1209-10 CE, was originally a slave who wielded considerable power in the royal house-hold and ultimately became the King. Had the Rehl (*Quran*-stand) in question been a forgery, it could not have been attributed to a king of the slave dynasty. A forgery is always attempted to raise the socio-economic context of an art-piece to fetch more value. In this case, the forger could not have achieved the same by attributing it to the name of a slave king. Besides, the over-all treatment, delineation of the floral motif, the old architectural pattern adopted for the lower portion of the book-stand and so also archaic characters of the script, which represent early evolutionary stage of Nastalique script, would collectively hint at its genuineness.

The foregoing discussion based on the Chinese, Central Asian and Indian sources would reveal that India possessed full-fledged hard-stone technology during 2nd-1st century BCE, if not earlier. A number of crystal reliquaries were found from the excavations of the Buddhist stupas which are datable to 2nd-1st century BCE. Robert Skelton supported this view by citing an example of a similar crystal reliquary which is shaped like goose and presently kept in the British Museum, London. According to Mho scale, crystal is harder stone than jade. Hence, it must not have been difficult for Indian artisans to carve jade by using the same tools and technology for working on jade. This accomplished hard-stone technology continued even during Early Medieval and Medieval Era to fashion jade-objects. It was the Indian missionaries who introduced this hard stone technology in Central Asia as and when they went there to propagate their faith in China via Central Asia.

Hence, it will be wrong to believe that Indians learnt the art of jade-carving from Central Asian, Persian or Chinese during seventeenth century CE.

References

1. John Irwin, 'Mughal Jades', *The Times of India Annual*, Bombay, 1968. John Irwin has opined that all early Jahangir Jades could be of Persian origin.
2. *Ibid.*
3. S.H. Hansford, *Chinese Carved Jades*, London, 1968, p. 97.
4. S. Beal, *Si-Yu-Ki: Buddhist Records of the Western World*, vol. 1, p. 89.
5. S.H. Hansford, *op. cit.*, 1968, p. 70.
6. Robert Skelton, *The Relations between the Chinese and Indian Jade Carving Traditions*, p. 100.
7. S.R. Sarma, "Historical Notices on Gem-Cutting in India", In: G. Kuppuram and K. Kumudamani (eds.), *History of Science and Technology in India*, vol. V, 1999, Delhi, pp. 144-145.
8. Irfan Habib, "Technology and Barriers to Social Change in Mughal India", *Indian Historical Review*, 1978-79, 1-2: 163.

9. John Fryer, A New Account of East India and Persia in Eight letters, being nine years travels, Begun 1672 and finished 1681 (London 1698), reprint, Delhi, 1985, p. 113.

10. Teng Shu-ping, *Catalogue of Special Exhibition of Hindustan Jade in the National Palace Museum,* Taipei, 1988, p. 77.

11. Lokesh Chandra, "The Cultural Linkage of India", *Citi Vithika,* 1999-2000, 5 (142): 50.

12. *Ibid.*

13. S. Beal, *op. cit.*, p. 21.

14. O.C. Gangoli, *Andhra Sculpture,* The Government of Andhra Pradesh, Hyderabad, 1973, pp. 8-9.

15. M.L. Nigam, "Khawasul Jawahara — Some Information on the History of Jade-Art of Central Asian Regions". In: S.D. Trivedi (ed.), *The Glorious Heritage of India,* pp. 111-115.

16. *Ibid.*

17. *Ibid.*

18. *Ibid.*

19. Teng Shu-ping, *op. cit.*

20. M.L. Nigam, "A Rare Jade Book-Stand of Sultanate Period", *Salar Jung Museum Bi-Annual Research Journal,* vol. IX-X, 1976-77.

Chapter 2

The Mughals Jades

Babar, a direct descendant of the Turkish ruler, Timur and also distantly related to Chingiz Khan from his mother's side, had reached India in 1526 CE. He was constantly engaged in battle-fields to expand his territories and hence, had little time to make any cultural contribution. Babar died in 1530 CE. Babar was succeeded by his son Humayun who was a weak and inexperienced ruler. He soon lost his empire to an Afghan Chief, Sher Shah Suri who chased him out of Agra. Humayun fled and took refuge in Persia. With the help of the Persian monarch, Shah Tahmasp, Humayun regained the throne of Delhi in 1555 CE. He however, did not survive for long and died in 1556, after falling from the steps of his library building in Purana Qila.

Humayun was succeeded by his son, Jalal-ud-din Mohammad Akbar, the most illustrious and successful ruler among the Indian Mughals. No doubt, the Mughal kings loved their Turkish lineage, they also admired Persian language and culture. It was, however, Akbar who encouraged Indian values and traditions which ultimately resulted in a soft blend and wonderful fusion of Indo-Persian cultural norms and traditions.

It is this harmonious blend of medieval Indian arts and culture which later reached its zenith during the Mughal rule in India. Akbar's main interest lied on Indian architecture. While planning to build a new capital at Fatehpur Sikri to honor the Sufi Saint, Sheikh Salim Chisti who had blessed him with the birth of three children, including Salim, Akbar invited the gifted artisans and skilled craftsman from Gujarat and Bengal to take up the work of construction. Gujarat was also famous for carving of both crystal and agate. The artisans of Gujarat could have used the same traditional tools and technology to fashion jade-objects also as crystal is harder stone than jade. The crystal *lingas* and images were produced in Gujarat at that time when Mughals had reached India. Thus the gifted artisans who were employed by Akbar to take up the work of construction of the new capital of Fatehpur Sikri might have also taken up the work of producing jade vessels to be used in Mughal household and court.

Akbar seems to have established there a royal workshop (*kharkhana*) also wherein hundreds of master craftsmen and artists, such as painters, weavers, jewellers, etc. worked to produce luxury items for the Mughal court. The jade vessels were also produced there and the same practice continued during Jahangir's rule also. A dark green jade wine jug, presently housed in the British Museum, London, is inscribed with the name of Jahangir and the date 1619 CE. It was made at Fathapur during the fourteenth regnal year of his reign. Fathapur can be identified with modern Fatehpur Sikri. The jade wine jug in question was fashioned (Murattab Shud) at Fatehpur Sikri. Apart from Fatehpur, the Mughal workshops were also functioning at Agra, Delhi and Lahore. Further, Mandu a provincial headquarter under the Mughals, also had a similar workshop which was busy producing jade vessels. The two jade wine cups, which are presently housed in Bharat Kala Bhavan, Varanasi were made at Mandu. The legends inscribed on both the cups mention the name of Mandu and the date in Hijri Era equivalent to 1617 CE (Pl. 4-5).

Jade Art under Akbar

It is now evident that the fancy jade-items were being produced by Indian artisans at several places during the period of Akbar and Jahangir. We do know of several inscribed and uninscribed jades which can safely be attributed to Akbar's period. For instance, a beautiful dagger with jade hilt, carved as a lion's head is now exhibited in the Salar Jung Museum, Hyderabad (Pl. 2). The legend in gold, "Amal-i-Saleh" reveals the name of the maker Saleh and the date in Hijri Era 1011 which is equivalent to 1602 CE. Akbar died in 1605 CE and hence, the dagger in question is datable to Akbar's period. The legend is carved on the back of the blade in Naskh Characters belonging to Akbar's time. The blade of the dagger has been carved out of a highly sophisticated watered steel which goes very well with jade hilt of the said dagger. The square face, open jaws, the protruding teeth on the two front sides, the cup-shaped ears and the tuft of the hair pleated on the lion's neck are the features similar to those found with the lion's depicted in early miniature paintings of Jahangir's period. The eyes and tongue of the lion are fashioned out of red rubies. The carving of the lion's head is in round, reminiscent of the early sculptural quality of the medieval era of Indian History.

Stephen Markel has raised doubt about the dating of the said dagger[1]. Markel himself admits that he has not seen the dagger. In fact, he came to Salar Jung Museum when the re-organization work of the jade-gallery was going on and some important jade-objects were sent to the stores for security reasons. However, if Markel had not seen the dagger, how could he arrive to such a decision. How could he judge the date of the hilt which he puts in mid seventeenth century. Hence, we may not agree with the opinion of Markel. We welcome him to come to Salar Jung Museum again and re-examine the art-object.

Another inscribed jade-object which can be attributed to Akbar's period is an archer's thumb ring, made of pale white jade. It bears an inscription giving the name of "Shah Salim" as the owner. It is now kept in the Bharat Kala Bhavan, Varanasi. The title "Shah Salim" would suggest that the archer's thumb ring was produced when Jahangir was only an heir-apparent and had not attained the throne. Akbar died in 1605 CE. Thus the thumb ring in question must have been made during Akbar's rule only. It has been suggested by some scholars that the thumb ring was possibly made at Allahabad during the period between 1599 and 1604 when Jahangir was camping there as a rebel against his father, Akbar. The traces of gold-inlay and the gem-setting to form an arabesque can still be seen as decorative device during Akbar's period.

Yet, another Indian jade specimen, though uninscribed, is a life-size tortoise presently housed in the British Museum, London (Pl. 3). The size of the jade tortoise, measuring 20" in length, bears distinctive quality of carving which is not found in other examples of Jahangir's jades. This unique specimen, very realistically carved of dark green nephrite, was found from the debris of a cistern near the confluence of the rivers, namely Ganga, Jamuna and Saraswati at Allahabad in India. It may not be out of context to mention here that the tortoise is said to be a mount of the River Goddess Jamuna in Hindu mythology. Was this unique jade piece made to be offered to river goddess, Jamuna at the Confluence in Allahabad? Otherwise, there can be no justification for it's being found in a cistern near the confluence at Allahabad. Further, it must also be mentioned here that the shape and size of this jade tortoise, unlike the jade turtles made in China during Ming period, represents a true Indian variety which is not to be found in China. Thus, the typical

Indian specie, it's find-spot, and traditional Indian mode of carving are adequate proof of its Indian origin. It can be dated to Akbar's period, even earlier.

Of late, some large jade plates have come to light from different museums of the world. These jade plates are quite heavy and their workmanship is somewhat, crude. One such large jade plate is presently housed in the National Museum, New Delhi. Another similar large jade plate is kept in the collection of the Cleveland Museum, USA. Both the plates are shaped like the Chinese porcelain plates which are found depicted in Mughal miniature paintings, particularly in the *Babar Nama* datable to ca. 1593 CE.

A careful scrutiny of the jades produced during Akbar's period would reveal the different forms and technique which are not to be found in the jades of subsequent periods. The life-size jade tortoise, the very realistically produced lion's head-shaped dagger exhibit a very sculpture like quality in bold carving. The traditional mode of Indian carving to cut away the background surface to produce decorative motifs was prevalent in India during Akbar's period. The traditional Indian mode of carving appears to have continued at the beginning of Jahangir's era also, though scarcely. A cup made of some jade-like material presently housed in Rhode Island School of Design Museum, is inscribed with the name of Jahangir and the date 1021 H, equivalent to 1613 CE. The flared walls of the cup are decorated with alternating cartouches containing flowering plants. The technique applied in fashioning the cup is the same traditional Indian technique which Indian artisans used in making stone-sculptures in ancient India.

Jade under Jahangir

It is now known beyond doubt that the art of jade-carving was fully in vogue during Akbar's period. Beautiful jade-objects were made both in the royal workshops and so also in other private centers to meet the growing public demand. Akbar took personal interest in the production of beautiful art-objects to be used in his court and also to be offered as royal gifts to his courtiers. Akbar had employed a number of Persian and Turanian artists to join his workshops.

Jahangir, son and successor of Akbar, had possibly inherited a rich legacy from his father to promote and preserve decorative arts, including jade art which he further encouraged. It is also probable that Jahangir might have inherited some very rare jade-objects from his father. An eye witness account is found from the records of an English sea-captain Hawkins who visited Agra in 1609 CE. There he reports that Jahangir, son of Akbar owned "Of *eshime* (Persian Yashm) which stone commeth from Cathaia, one battman" (i.e. 55 pounds weight) and "Of drinking cuppes five hundred,fifty very riche, that is to say, made of one piece of ballace ruby, and also of emerods, of *eshim* (jade) of Turkish stone, and of other sorts of stones".[2]

Jahangir ascended the throne in 1605 CE. It could not have been possible for him to get such a large number of wine cups made of jade and other precious stones within a period of four years, when the English Captain, Hawkins visited Agra in 1609 CE. It would suggest that the art of jade-carving was fully in vogue in India when Jahangir ascended the throne in 1605 CE.

The first jade wine cup inscribed with the name of Jahangir and the date 1016 in Hijri Era corresponding to 1607-08 CE is presently housed in the Brooklyn Museum, New York. The cup is carved out of mottled green nephrite. It is decorated with three bands of inscriptions with three pairs of horizontal lines. The central inscription in Tughra form in Suls characters mentions that the said cup attained completion by the command of his majesty.... Mohammed Jahangir during 2nd regnal year in 1016 A.H. (corresponding to 1607-08 CE). Thus the cup in question was made in the royal workshops just after two years when Jahangir occupied the throne in 1605 CE. No doubt, the cup exhibits the Persian impact which had reached India earlier during Sultanate period. However, the Persian and Chinese impact, which is found very dominating at the beginning of Jahangir's rule, did not last long. The Indian artisans soon overcame it by introducing beautiful organic forms and motifs which made the Indian jade-art more attractive and colourful. The emergence of the floral arabesque in its multiple forms in Jahangir's architecture and decorative arts such as stone, textile and jewellery etc., became very effective in bringing the alien influence to background. The inlay of gold and silver wire on the glossy surface of the jade to depict variety of floral motifs and forms became the main decorative device to attract the eye of the beholder.

The second known jade wine cup of Jahangir, made of dark green nephrite, is presently housed in Victoria and Albert Museum, London. It has shallow carved walls, small ring foot and a handle-shaped as peacock's head. The other handle is missing. There is a short inscription in the central cartouches which reads that the cup was made during the eighth regnal year of the emperor, Jahangir in the year 1022 A.H.; equivalent to 1613-14 CE. The beautiful symmetrical form, the exquisite workmanship and the dark green colour of the stone have led Robert Skelton, to believe that the cup itself is almost certainly pre-Mughal, and is probably late Timurid or early safavid work. However, the lotus motif carved in relief at the interior of the bowl, is a positive evidence of its Indian origin. The Indian lapidaries of seventeenth century were quite competent to produce a beautiful jade cup.

The lotus has been an important motif of Indian art right from its inception. A well-known example is the begging bowl of Buddha which is presently kept in the National Museum, Kabul.

It is an excellent piece made of grey granite stone with the delicately chiselled as full blown lotus flower. The said begging bowl was given by Buddha himself to the people of Vaishali when he was leaving for Kushinagar to attain *Mahaparinirvan.* The great Kushan king, Kanishka who promoted Buddhism, brought this bowl from Vaishali to his capital, Purushpura (mod. Peshawar) and then to Gandhara (mod. Kandahar). The Chinese Buddhist pilgrims, Fahien and Hiuen-T'sang have also documented this bowl in their travelogues which speak about its authenticity. It is thus evident that the lotus has been an important motif in Indian art right from its inception. In 1980, the Afghan President Najibullah brought the bowl to Kabul Museum where it is kept now

The other two inscribed jade wine cups of Jahangir, as stated earlier, are presently kept in Bharat Kala Bhavan, Varanasi. Inscriptions on both the cups mention that they were made at Mandu during the twelfth regnal year of Jahangir in 1026 A.H., which would mean in 1617 CE. One of these two jade wine cups is made of dark green nephrite in the shape of full blown lotus with its petals carved on the outer surface in low relief.[3] The Persian inscription in gold is written in good Nastalique over the carved lotus petals. It reads "special cup, which is antidote to poison (Pa-Zahar) was made for Jahangir, the son of Akbar, at Mandu in 1026 A.H., equivalent to 1617 CE. The present lotus cup heralds the beginning of new trend to create jade-vessels in organic forms such as leaves, buds and flowers right from 1617 CE. This new trend reached its zenith during the rule of Mughal emperor, Shah Jahan.

The second jade wine cup of Jahangir, made at Mandu in 1617 CE, is made of white Jade. It is also housed in Bharat Kala Bhavan, Varanasi (Pl. 5). It is carved in bold relief. The twining stems, curling leaves and the lobed handle are typical characteristics of the Chinese art of late Ming period. The cup has however, been attributed to Indian workmanship for two reasons. Firstly, the workmanship is quite crude as compared to the Chinese type of carving. Its coarse modelling and crude workmanship, contrary to the fine treatment and smooth carving of the Chinese jade workmanship, would suggest the possibility of its being made in India after some Chinese prototype. Further a lotus and leaf pattern found carved at the inner bottom of the cup would confirm its Indian origin.[4]

Apart from jade wine cups, the royal lapidaries of Jahangir also fashioned some other interesting items of jade, such as the wine jugs, amulets, an inkpot and tiny jade phials which are found scattered in various museums and private collections of the world. We have already made a mention of a jade wine jug, which according to its legend carved at the rim, was made (Murattab shud) during the fourteenth regnal year of Jahangir at Fatehpur Sikri. The jug can thus be dated to 1619 CE. Had it been made in Persia or elsewhere, there was no need for the scribe to mention that the jug was made at Fathapur. Another jade specimen belonging to Jahangir is an inkpot, presently housed in the Metropolitan Museum at New York.[5] It is carved out of dark green jade and provided with a gold lid and a chain. A Persian inscription in good Nastaliq reads, "The form of inkpot attained completion (Surat Itmam Yafta) for emperor Jahangir" (son of) Akbar during fourteenth regnal year, equivalent to 1619 CE. The name of the maker, "Amal-e-Momin Jahangiri" is also mentioned which would suggest that the artist, Momin who made this jade inkpot, was employed in the royal workshop (*karkhana*) of emperor Jahangir (Pl. 6).

Yet, another scholar, A.S. Melikian – Chirvani attributes the workmanship of early jades, inscribed with the name of the Mughal emperor Jahangir, to Saida Gilani who was the head of the Goldsmith workshop (darughe-ye zargar Khanae) of Jahangir. Saida Gilani, who was a distinguished poet, calligrapher, a gem engraver and jeweller, had left Iran for Hindustan and ultimately joined the Mughal workshop under Jahangir who greatly admired him. According to Assadullah S.M. Chirvani, the three early jade vessels of Jahangir, viz. a jade wine cup dated in 1016 H (1607-08 CE), presently housed in Brooklyn Museum, the second jade wine cup dated in 1022 H (1613-14 CE) now in the Victoria and Albert Museum, London and the wine jug, dated in 1028 (1618-19 CE) which is presently exhibited in the British Museum, London, were fashioned by Saida Gilani. His hypothesis is based on the metallic shape of objects and calligraphic decoration. To quote him, "This conjunction irresistibly calls to mind the name of Saida Gilani the poet. His participation in the execution of the cup as the gem cutter, that he was, would account for the unique emphasis on pure calligraphy and for its obviously Iranian Character." Pointing out certain common features in all the aforesaid three jade vessels; he further writes, "Taken together, these analogies point to Saida Gilani as the likely maker". While appreciating his profound knowledge of Persian poetry and Islamic calligraphy, we may not agree with his present surmise. Firstly, it lacks positive evidence, both literal and epigraphic to suggest that Saida Gilani was the artist who made the aforesaid three jade-vessels for Jahangir. Secondly, tools and technology for carving jade which is harder than steel, are totally different than those of Goldsmith's art. Neither Jahangir nor Saida Gilani himself ever mention his name in this regard, though he is often mentioned as expert in the field of jewel making. We do know the names of "Saleh" and "Momin Jahangiri" as expert jade-carvers who worked in the imperial jade-workshop and whose names are found engraved on exquisite jade-objects which they had made for the royal use. Had Saida Gilani fashioned exquisite jade pieces for the Mughal emperors, Jahangir and Shah Jahan, he would certainly mention his name along with the owners name to be inscribed on such objects. So far the old Persian metal forms, Persian poetry and calligraphic ornamentation are concerned, these had become familiar with Indian artisan even prior to the Mughal advent in India. The same could be reproduced by them as and when the occasion arose to do so. It is thus difficult to agree with his arguments which are more of speculation devoid of any positive historical evidence.

An inscribed jade, *huqqa* with small mango-shaped apple green base and the pipe and chillam, made of jade with the silver mounts around the body, is another specimen attributed to Jahangir. It is now kept in the National Museum, New Delhi. Inscriptions on silver mounts in chaste Persian, mention the date 1032 A.H. corresponding to 1621 CE. The inverted lotus pattern of the upper base, the open workmanship (*jali*) around the pedestal and flawless carving are suggestive of its early Mughal art style. Scholars, however, have expressed doubt about the authenticity of the inscription on the ground that Jahangir was against tobacco smoking and therefore, the jade *huqqa* need not be attributed to Jahangir. Yet, we must not forget that Jahangir was equally addicted to other intoxicants, like hashish and opium. The *huqqa* might have been used to smoke some other similar substance.

There are two almost identical bud-shaped perfume Phials carved out of white jade with elongated petals emerging from a ring of sepals. Both the Phials carry an identical Persian inscription around the top, giving the name of the emperor, Jahangir, and the date in Hijiri Era, which can be translated as follows, "by order of king Jahangir (son of King Akbar) (undeciphered) jade, Regnal year 21, 1036 A.H. (1626 27)". One of the two phials is exhibited in Chhatrapati Shivaji Maharaj Vastu Sangrahalaya, Mumbai (Pl. 7) and the other lies in the State Museum, Lucknow. It is quite likely that both the jade phials were made to order for Jahangir by one and the same artist.

The few early jades produced at the beginning of Jahangir's reign exhibit strong Persian impact. The forms of these early Jade vessels are drawn from the Persian metal ware. Secondly, the decorative device showing calligraphic panels running horizontally in parallel rows at the neck of the bowls and cups, is also adopted from the Persian model. This similarity of forms and the chased inscriptional device led some scholars to presume that the Indian learnt the art of jade-carving from Persia during Jahangir period. However, this Persian impact was soon overcome by Indian artists by introducing indigenous organic forms, such as the leaves, fruits, flowers in their decorative art. In fact, the strong Persian impact on early art of jade-carving at the beginning of Jahangir's period should be accounted for the eclectic quality of Mughal art. We have already mentioned that a number of Iranian and Turanian artisans in Mughal court-workshops worked right from the Akbar's period. It should not have been difficult for the Iranian artisans to introduce certain Persian elements in early Mughal jade art of Jahangir period.

Jades under Shah Jahan

The long, unsurpassed power and prosperity during Shah Jahan's reign added to the pristine glory and grandeur of the Mughal art and architecture. His ardent love for white colour, organic forms and thin, sensuous carving are truly reflected in Taj Mahal, an epitome for his beloved wife, Mumtaz Mahal. The wide spread popularity of India as golden bird in the west prompted several reputed scholars, jewellers and artisans to flock to India and join the Mughal court where they worked along with Indian Muslim and Hindu craftsmen which made the Mughal art eclectic in its real sense. The artists of the Shah Jahan's court were gifted with rare creative vision, artistic precision and aesthetic sensibilities. They drew inspiration from Indian soil, assimilated alien trends and traditions to enrich their own fabric and ultimately led the art to its perfection. No doubt, Shah Jahan's prime interest was in architecture. He, however, paid equal attention to decorative arts including jade art. He showered his love on Indian jewels and jewellery also. Besides, the magical and medicinal qualities attributed to jade might also have led Mughal nobility to patronize jade-art. For example, jade was also called "Pa-Zahar" which means antidote to poison. It led to the production of jade-vessel, including drinking wine cups, in large numbers. The wearing of jade on the body was considered as a cure for the heart, kidney, and other ailments. It gave incentive to fashion jade ornaments. Jade stone was also popularly considered auspicious to gain victory in battle-fields. This is why, we find a good number of swords and daggers with their hilts made of jade. All these factors must have helped the production of beautiful jade objects during the period of Shah Jahan.

There are only a few inscribed jade specimens which can be attributed to the Mughal emperor, Shah Jahan. The first item, a jade archer's thumb ring of Shah Jahan is made of dark green jade with an inscription in gold. It reads, "Sahib-e-Qiran-i-Sani," a title of Shah Jahan, which he had adopted to emulate his ancestor, Timur (Pl. 8). The date given in the fourth regnal year is 1040 A.H. equivalent to 1631 CE. It is housed in the Salar Jung Museum, Hyderabad. Another archer's ring of Shah Jahan, made of white jade, is presently kept in the Victoria and Albert Museum, London. Here, the date 1042 A.H., equivalent to 1632 CE, is given along with the above mentioned title of the emperor. Again, there is a heart-shaped, inscribed pendant made of white nephrite in the Al-Sabah collection in Kuwait National Museum, which gives the name of Shah Jahan and also the date in 10th regnal year, viz. 1047 A.H. (1637 CE). A similar white jade pendant in Bharat Kala Bhavan, Varanasi is dated in the fourteenth regnal year of Shah Jahans's reign in 1051 A.H. (1641 CE). Though the name of the emperor is not given here yet, it's beautiful form seems to have been fashioned for the emperor only.

A jade wine cup, shaped as a halved turban gourd and bearing an inscription in cartouches reads, "Article of the king of kings, the world conqueror, Shah Jahan, the second Lord of the conjunction" and the date is mentioned in 21st regnal year, 1057 A.H., equivalent to 1647 CE. The cup is made of mottled green nephrite with prominent ribs over the body. The rib-moulding symmetrically reaches the rim and then forms a stem of two pairs of leaves resembling scrolling half-palmette which meet opposite the turban projection where the stem joins the gourd. The foot of the cup is made of five overlapping spear-shaped leaves.

There seems to have existed a practice in the Mughal lapidaries to produce copies of choicest jade-specimens made for the royalty. We have already discussed two exactly similar tiny jade bottles (phials) which bear similar form and inscription giving the name of Mughal emperor, Jahangir and the date 1036 A.H. (1626-27 CE). Similarly the above mentioned jade wine-cup of Shah Jahan, presently kept in British Museum, London, was made and inscribed after his name in 1057 A.H. (1647 CE). There are two other known copies of this particular jade wine-cup of Shah Jahan, one in Asian Art Museum, San Francisco in USA and the other in private collection in U.K. The former does not bear the name of the emperor yet, inscription in Persian language reads. "Drink at the order of Allah". The latter one is also inscribed but in Turkish language. It would thus suggest that the jade specimens of Mughal Era travelled far and wide in view of their beauty and artistic excellence. The cup bearing a Turkish inscription must have been inscribed at a later date.

Another jade wine cup of Shah Jahan, now in the Victoria and Albert Museum, London, is a masterpiece of the jade workmanship of the Mughal India. The cup in question is fashioned out of the milky white jade as halved gourd, which tapers symmetrically to the handle in the form of a realistically carved wild goat's head. It rests on a foot formed of lotus petals and acanthus leaves. The inscription mentions the title "Sahib-e-Qiran-i-Sahi" and the date 1067 A.H., equivalent to 1657 CE. The thin sensuous carving, the milky white jade and the glossy surface, the realistically fashioned wild goat's head and the lotus base with stylized acanthus leaves around are executed with perfect symmetry and form. This cup is, no doubt, the finest specimen of the Mughal jade workmanship of India (Pl. 9).

The most remarkable quality of the carved jades of Shah Jahan's period is their thin and sensuous carving. While considering the hardness of the stone and the primitive tools and manual jade-carving, it is somewhat amazing to note the flawless execution of exquisite organic forms of the wine cups shaped as flowers, fruits and leaves carved in their natural thinness. Even the veins over leaves and flowers have been successfully brought to exhibit their realistic nature. The close observation of nature by the artisans of Shah Jahan's reign is further reflected in the treatment of curling leaves where the tip is slightly twisted and raised from the ground by chiselling out the space beneath it. The ingenuity and dexterity of carving remains unsurpassed where the stone is found melting like wax to produce the desired forms under the skilled hands of the artisans who had gained complete control and mastery over the medium.

Another notable characteristic of the art of jade-carving of Shah Jahan's reign is its eclectic quality. It was during this period that the reputation of India as a Golden Bird had gone far and wide. The well-known scholars, architects and artisans from distant lands and regions flocked to the Mughal court to win royal favour. Apart from the Persian and Central Asian artists, there were a large number of Europeans also who worked for the Mughal court. A Venetian expert, Niccolas Manucci, who remained in India till 1717 CE reported that as far back as the reign of Akbar there were many Europeans working in Mughal court as "lapidars, enamellers, goldsmiths, surgeons and gunners. Similarly the famous lapidary Hortensio Bronzoni worked for Shah Jahan and Aurangzeb until his death at Agra in 1677 CE. Thus, jade-carving of Shah Jahan's age exhibits a wonderful fusion of the Persian, Central Asian and European artistic norms and traditions combined with those of the traditional Indian workmanship. The famous wine cup of Shah Jahan in the Victoria and Albert Museum, London, inscribed and dated in 1067 A.H. (1657 CE) is a clear cut example. Here, the gourd-shaped form of the cup in question is likely to have been derived from the earlier Chinese art. The wild goat's head-shaped hilt and the acanthus leaves clasped underneath are probably the Venetian influence. The thin sensuous carving, the lotus petal base and the lustrous polish exhibit the true characteristics of the Indian jade art of Shah Jahan's period. The famous cup, of Shah Jahan, which lies in the collection of Victoria and Albert Museum, London, is an example to bear the quality of eclecticism of Mughal art.

Another distinctive quality of the jade-art of Shah Jahan's period is the floral decorative device. The artisans of Shah Jahan had a passion for floral depiction in various forms, such as arabesque, flowers emerging from pots, flower vases arranged in rows, both horizontally and vertically.

It is needless to emphasize that the art of jade-carving in India had reached its zenith during the reign of Shah Jahan. The most intricate and flawless carving, the successful execution of the subtle naturalistic forms, their realistic treatment, lustrous polish and unique decorative devices are simply superb. The spontaneous growth of form, the thin and sensuous carving the striking contours and rhythmic line left no scope for further improvement in the art of jade-carving. The later artisans of the subsequent periods were left with little room to make further development in the art, except the lavish use of gold and precious stones which became the characteristic feature of the jade specimens of the late eighteenth and nineteenth centuries in India. The art of jade-carving of Shah Jahan's period not only reached its zenith but it also brought an international recognition to Indian jade craftsmanship.

Jade under Aurangzeb (1657-1707 CE)

In spite of the fact that, Aurangzeb extended his empire over Deccan by conquering Bijapur and Golkonda in 1686-87 CE, there seems to have a sudden decline in realm of Indian Fine Arts. Certain scholars believe that Aurangzeb, due to his strict religious orthodoxy, did not fully subscribe to the development of fine arts, such as paintings, music and dance etc., Even though his predecessors, viz. Akbar, Jahangir and Shah Jahan wore costly robes and jewellery, Aurangzeb used the simple dress and ornaments which were prescribed by the religious injunctions. His court-historian, Muhammad Kazim, who wrote *Alamgir Namah,* informs us that the emperor had even discarded the use of gold for making his personal jewellery.[6] Instead, he preferred jade for fashioning the ornaments which were deemed to be in full conformity with the Islamic faith. It would suggest that the art of jade-carving did not lose its importance during Aurangzeb's rule. Further, the example set by the emperor must also have prompted the Mughal nobility to use jade ornaments which provided extra impetus to jade art.

There are a number of known daggers with their hilts made of jade, which are inscribed with the name of Aurangzeb. A dagger with the fine watered steel blade and the hilt carved as bunch of flower buds and made of milky white jade is presently housed in the Salar Jung Museum, Hyderabad. The legend inscribed on the blade in gold letters reads "This dagger of Aurangzeb by good fortune, the dagger of Alamgir (Aurangzeb) is the key of the many kingdoms". It measures (26.5 cm blade) (12.1 cm hilt) (43.2 cm general). The blade is inscribed with the date 1072 A.H. (1661-1662 CE) (Pl. 10).

Yet another dagger with a hilt made of pale green jade and shaped in the form of horse's head is housed in the Los Angeles County Museum of Art. An inscription on the blade provides the date in Hijra year, 1071 A.H. which is equivalent to 1660-1661 CE. Another dagger with an ivory hilt is presently housed in National Museum, New Delhi. Another dagger made of deep gray-blue jade and the hilt is shaped as Nilgai's head, is also exhibited in the Metropolitan Museum of Art, New York, measures 38.1 cm.

Main Characteristics of Mughal Jade-Art

The two important characteristics, viz. the eclecticism and organic forms of the bowls and cups, begin to appear right from the reign period of Jahangir. It was, however, left to the visionary artisans of Shah Jahan to lead these decorative devices to perfection. The artisans of Shah Jahan's court were great lovers of nature and their close observation, resulted in maximum beauty and refinement of the Mughal art. Yet, another interesting quality of Mughal art under Shah Jahan is the exact similarity between the decorative motifs and designs, as found depicted, both in Mughal architecture as well as decorative art objects.

To further highlight this point, Jagdish Mittal, a well-known scholar has shown in one of his articles that the master painters of each school of painting prepared designs (*charbas*) to be used in the objects of decorative art, including metal ware, jewellery arms and armour, carpets, textiles, glass and stone, including jade.[7] The floral motifs and designs on the walls of Taj Mahal are virtually identical in style of those carved on the objects of decorative arts. It is same with the objects of jade belonging to late Mughal Era. There remained a continuous flow of Indian jades through Sinkiang on their way to Peking. Many carvan merchants brought them to Yarkand which was the main market for Indian jade. From Yarkand, they were taken to the Chinese emperor, as gifts by the officials of the Chinese army personnel who were posted there. The local Muslim Chiefs also sent jade objects as tributes to the emperor to gain royal favour. These jade merchants were locally called "Tu-wan".[8] With a view to encourage jade-trade with India, the Chinese emperor Ch'ien-lung had granted tax-exemption to the Indian jade merchants who, as mentioned in imperial verses, were making 300% profit.

Although, the Indian Jade-trade with China had existed earlier also yet, it was the great liking by Chinese emperor, Ch'ien-lung who provided fresh momentum to the trade. He uses a number of metaphors and similes to describe the aesthetic beauty and technical ability of Indian jade carvers. The Chinese emperor greatly loved Indian jades for a number of reasons. Praising the thin and sensuous carving, he describes the Indian jade specimens as "Paper thin". Their wafer thinness made them very light and the emperor describes it, "refined of manufacture" or "better than painting". This quality of thin sensuous carving is well reflected in a peepal leaf-shaped wine cup, no. XLIX-219 which is presently kept in the Salar Jung Museum, Hyderabad (Pl. 11). He further extolled another quality of Hindustan jade which included "extreme refinement" and sensitive thinness whose lustrous polish left no traces of the carving. Again, he emphasizes the carving in low relief, which covered the vessel surface with masses of acanthus leaves and lotus flowers. According to Teng-shu-ping, these motifs created a layered effect that sometimes gave the impression of having more depth than there actually was". In his verse 73, the Chinese emperor says, "One sees the flowers and leaves but feels no trace of them".[9]

Expressing his over-all appreciation for Indian Jades, the emperor often declares in his poems that such exceptional craftsmanship of Indian jade carvers surpassed the best works of the Chinese jade-artists of Soochow.[10]

The abnormal increase in the jade-trade with the eastern world did prove to be a major incentive for Indian jade-carvers to introduce new organic forms and fresh technical devices in their works so as to enrich their art and make it more attractive to their foreign buyers. A good number of such jade-vessels and other utilitarian objects, datable to the eighteenth and nineteenth centuries are found in the collections of various museums and art-galleries of the world.

The very thin, translucent carving of the jade vessels by the Indian jade-carvers, which has been immensely admired by the Chinese ruler, Ch'ien-lung in his commemorative verses, was not a sudden development during eighteenth century CE. This trend appears to have begun during the period of Mughal emperor, Shah Jahan. A close scrutiny of the actual objects which are contemporaneous to Shah Jahan would confirm this point. A very beautiful, thinly carved jade wine cup (no. XLIX-217) in the collection of Salar Jung Museum, Hyderabad is a fine example of this new trend. It has a lobed form like a halved gourd. A leaf is tapering towards the stem. The bowl has several lobes which converge towards the stem to form the handle of the cup (Pl. 12).

An identical cup, made of milky white jade, is also housed in the Victoria and Albert Museum, London (Skeleton 1982: fig. 357). Yet another identical cup is also housed in Salar Jung Museum, Hyderabad (no. XLIX-230) (Pl. 13). There are several other jade wine cups such as leaf-shaped wine cup made of white jade, shaped like halved gourd with a leaf emerging from beneath to form a handle. Dated to seventeenth century CE (courtesy: Salar Jung Museum, Hyderabad) (no. XLIX-216) (Pl. 14).

A very thinly carved, leaf-shaped jade cup with its lobed bud-shaped handle emerging from beneath and joining the rim to form a handle, seventeenth century, Salar Jung Museum, Hyderabad (no. XLIX-582) (Pl. 15).

Similarly the use of gold and precious stones to decorate jade objects is very scarce during the time of Akbar and Jahangir. There are only few exceptions. For example the, lion-headed dagger, belonging to Akbar's period is now in the Salar Jung Museum, Hyderabad. It is earliest Indian Jade object where the head of the lion is provided with the tongue and eyes made of red ruby. The other exception is an archer's thumb ring of Jahangir which has traces of gold inlay and use of gems to form an arabesque. The stones are now missing. It is presently kept in Bharat Kala Bhavan, Varanasi. The practice of using gold and precious gems to decorate the jade appears to have begun right from the time of the Mughal emperor, Shah Jahan. A beautiful jade plate, showing the poppy flower design in gold and is inlaid with garnet is beautiful jade specimen can be dated to Shah Jahan period (1627-1658) (Pl. 16). It is housed in Chhatrapati Shivaji Maharaj Vastu Sangrahalaya, Mumbai. Another beautiful example is a leaf-shaped jade spice box (no. XLIX-199), kept in the Salar Jung Museum, Hyderabad. The entire cover of the box is beautifully studded with precious stones representing a plant with the leaves made of dark green emeralds and flowers made of dark red rubies. It can safely be dated to seventeenth century CE, Mughal India (no. XLIX-199) (Pl. 17).

Further a dagger and a fruit knife (no. XLIX-311 and XLIX-312) are kept in the jade collection of Salar Jung Museum, Hyderabad. The butt-shaped white jade hilt of dagger is very richly studded with very dark emeralds as leaves and flowers are made of very dark red rubies (Pl. 18). The hilt of the fruit knife is shaped like the head of a parrot which is carved out of a single ruby. The hilt of the dagger attached with a bejwelled disc seventeenth century Mughal (Pl. 19).

It has already been mentioned that the Mughal emperor, Aurangzeb preferred jade stones against gold for his personal jewellery. This was possibly the beginning of the use of jade jewellery for the Mughal nobility. A very beautiful bejwelled jade pendant with gold inlay representing floral motifs with eight leaves emerging from the centre, having a big topaz-shaped as a centre flower. The flowers on the right side are made of a dark red rubies. There is a gold border all around, seventeenth century, Mughal (Pl. 20).

Yet another pendant is made of jade with gold inlay. The flowers are made of rubies. The vase is made of blue Sapphire, datable eighteenth century, Mughal India (Pl. 21). Jade bowl, inlaid with gems (Pl. 22). A dark green jade box inlaid in gold, eighteenth century CE (Pl. 23). A jade box decorated with beautiful enamelling workmanship, datable eighteenth century (Pl. 24).

The art of enameling was an inseparable part of the Mughal jewellery. Enamelling was also practice on jade to beautify the objects. A very beautiful jade mirror back in the jade collection of Salar Jung Museum, Hyderabad, is a master piece of jade enamelling work, eighteenth century, Mughal (no. XLIX-110) (Pl. 25).

There are numerous techniques practiced in studding of jewels, viz., by sticking of a gem into its appropriate socket with lac, by hammering it into the socket provided with a bed of gold or silver foil, and by setting the gem within provided layers of gold foil around to hold it firmly. While greatly admiring the unparalleled skill of Indian lapidaries, Birdwood remarks, "Their work is really manual and grows up spontaneously like a growing flower under their hands".[11]

References

1. Stephen Markel, "Inception and Maturation in Mughal Jades", *Marg*, 1992, 44 (2): 55.

2. W. Foster, *Early Travels in India,* Oxford, 1921, pp. 102-103.
3. Robert Skelton, *The Indian Heritage : Court Life and Arts Under Mughal Rule,* 1982, fig. 351.
4. Grace Morley, "On Applied Arts of India in Bharat Kala Bhavan", *Chhavi,* Golden Jubilee Volume.
5. A.S. Melikian-Chirvani, "Sa ida-ye Gilani and the Iranian Style Jades of Hindustan", *Bulletin of the Asia Institute,* New Series/ vol. 13, 1999.
6. Munshi Muhammad Kazim, "Alamgir Namah", *Royal Asiatic Society,* Calcutta, 1868, p. 1072.
7. Jagdish Mittal, "Indian Painters as Designers of Decorative Art Objects Mughal Period", In: M.L. Nigam (ed.), *Decorative Arts of India,* p. 129.
8. Teng-Shu-Ping, *Catalogue of a Special Exhibition of Hindustan Jade in the National Palace Museum,* Taipei (Taiwan), p. 89.
9. *Ibid.*
10. *Ibid.*
11. George C.M. Birdwood, *The Industrial Arts of India,* p. 175.

Chapter 3

Jades under Later Mughals (18th-19th century CE) and its Trade with China via Sinkiang

There existed a good deal of controversy about the origin of large number of Indian Jades of 18th-19th century, CE which are presently housed in various museums and art-galleries of the world, such as the Palace Museum, Peking in China, the National Palace Museum, Taipei, Taiwan, British Museum and Victoria and Albert Museum, London, Seattle Art Museum, Washington, Metropolitan Museum of Art, New York, Los Angeles County Museum of Art, Los Angeles, the Al-Sabah Collection in Kuwait and Topkapi Saray Museum in Turkey, etc.

In India, the largest quality collection of such jade-objects are presently housed mainly in Salar Jung Museum, Hyderabad, Bharat Kala Bhavan, Varanasi, Chhatrapati Shivaji Maharaj Vastu Sangrahalaya (formerly called Prince of Wales Museum), Mumbai, State Museum, Hyderabad, State Museum, Lucknow and the private Singhania Collection, Mumbai, etc.

These utilitarian Jade-objects can broadly be divided in two separate categories, viz., the food vessels and the miscellaneous objects. The food vessels include bowls, cups, plates, scoops, ladles, vases, jugs and pots to hold drinks and the other eatables. Among the miscellaneous category, there are jars, flasks, boxes, pen-cases, lampstands, censers book-stands, mirror frames, gun powder flasks, huqqa mohnals, hilts of swords and daggers, zafar takias, back-scratchers, jewellery pendants which were used by the Mughal nobility.

Technically speaking, all such Jades are exhibited with the typical Indian characteristic features, such as the thin sensuous carving, organic forms, lustrous polish and decorative motifs and designs belonging to Shah Jahan period. Even the inlay of gold and silver wires and the studding of the precious gems on the glossy surface of jade to delineate leaves, fruits and flowers are also typical of the early Mughal art. Further, the stylized motifs, such as the rosettes, quatrefoils and diamond motifs carved in low relief are similar to those of the Shah Jahan period.

Apart from the above mentioned characteristics, some of these jade specimens belonging to late seventeenth to nineteenth centuries also bear certain Chinese devices, such as the loose rings and lobes which are not found in traditional Indian art. Another interesting feature is the Chinese verses inscribed on the surface of some of these Jade items. These are in fact, the commemorative verses composed by the Chinese ruler, Ch'ien-lung in appreciation of such jade-objects as and when they came to him as tribute or gifts either from the Moslem Begs or from the Chinese officials posted in Sinkiang region.

Prior to the publication of the Catalogue of Special Exhibition of Hindustan Jade in the National Palace Museum, Taipei in 1983, there existed a good deal of confusion among scholars about the origin of all such jades which we have described above. The scholars held divergent views about the place of origin of all such jade specimens. The Chinese scholars had labelled them as "Indian School Jades" which were made in China for Indian market. Robert Skelton one of the pioneers to have worked on this subject, believed that "most of the so-called "Indian School" Jades are quite certainly Chinese for they merely apply misunderstood Indian motifs to Chinese shapes or employ Chinese devices such as lobes and loose rings which are not found in true Indian work".[1] This view does not hold good now after the publication of the verses composed by the Chinese ruler, Ch'ien-lung wherein he specifically describes all such jades to be of Indian origin.

Theory of Turkish Origin

In one of his learned papers presented at the fifth International Congress of Turkish Art, Skelton has attributed some of these jade specimens belonging to eighteenth and nineteenth centuries to Turkish workmanship. He writes, "Having recapitulated the state of our knowledge, as it was after the III Congress, I would like now to discuss several types of jade-objects which present very different devices and which hitherto tended to be attributed to Indian or to Chinese Craftsmen working in the Mughal style. Superficially these do resemble Mughal works, but I wish to put forward reasons for believing that they are of Turkish Origin".[2] In support of his argument, Skeleton puts forth the following Characteristics which according to him should be associated with the Turkish jade workmanship of late eighteenth to nineteenth century. These are "Twining stems and smooth edged leaves in relief decoration, flat horizontal and vertical handles, triangular or heart-shaped forms in bowls, stylized low relief decoration with "scooped" floral and leaf forms and in general a more formal and hard-edged character that we see in Mughal works".[3]

Robert Skeleton, in one of his learned paper, "characteristics of later Turkish jade carving"[4] has referred to certain floral motifs found on some so-far known as Mughal jades of India.

In support of his surmise, Skeleton has referred to a white jade jar, presently housed in the Victoria and Albert Museum, London. It has the decorative motif of the twining stems below the vessel which the emperor described in his Verses as "serpents". According to Skeleton, stems of this kind are not a feature of Mughal jade art and hence, he describes the jade jar in Victoria and Albert Museum to be of Turkish origin. In this regard, we may mention to a Poppy blossom bowl which is carved with a similar motif "twining stem" forming the foot of the vessel, which is housed in the Seattle Art Museum, Washington.

While describing this twining stem motif, James C.Y. Watt has remarked, "However, Mughal style was an eclectic one from the beginning, and there is no absolute reason why a feature of Chinese jade-carving popular since the sixteenth century should not have been incorporated in certain Mughal pieces, especially given the possibility that they were made for the Chinese market, or even carved with Ch'ien-lung in mind".[5]

Further, the scholars who did not consider these objects to be of Indian origin, gave two reasons in support of their hypothesis. Firstly, they believed that due to the strong religious leanings of the Mughal emperor, Aurangzeb, Indian arts, such as the miniature paintings, dance and music etc., received a major setback and under such adverse conditions it was not possible for Indian jade-carvers to produce such a large amount of jade objects. Secondly, the economy of the Mughal empire after the demise of Aurangzeb had dwindled down and thereby affected the Mughal nobility so adversely that it must have become very difficult for them to patronize Indian jade artists and jade-art. With such an apathetic market in India, the growing production of "Indian school jades" in China must be attributed to some other stimulus than the prospect of supplying Indian importers, wrote Skelton.[6]

The above remarks are partly true. No doubt, disturbed political conditions in north India after the death of Mughal emperor, Aurangzeb had greatly affected the socio-economic stability of the region. However, the working of the Indian arts and crafts did not cease to exist. Indian miniature paintings continued to flourish and so was the case with the art of Indian jade-carving. As we have already mentioned above, Muhammad Kazim, the court historian of Aurangzeb, mentions that the emperor had discarded the use of gold for making his jewellery as the wearing of gold, is prohibited in Islam. Instead, Aurangzeb recommended jade for making royal jewellery items. The example set by emperor must have prompted the Mughal nobility to follow the emperor by preferring jade for their personal ornaments. It was a great incentive for Indian jade-carvers to pursue their art more vigorously. As the French traveller, Bernier, who remained at Delhi during Aurangzeb's period, informs us that the artisans were actively engaged in producing fancy items of jade for the use of the Mughal court and Mughal nobility. He further says that jade was held in high esteem at the court of the Mughal rulers. Cups and other vessels are made of which I have some in my possession, most superbly gilt, and of peculiar manufacture. It is an eye-witness account given by a French traveller who was in Delhi at that time and hence cannot be doubted.

Yet another source which goes to confirm the statement of Bernier about the flourishing of the jade art are the commemorative verses composed by the Chinese emperor Ch'ien-lung, some of which are found inscribed on the surface of the jade vessels which reached him either through gifts or purchase. Referring to the jade-trade between India and China, he remarks, "Hindustan is located to the south-west of Mount

Patako and east of Afghanistan. Their artists excel at jade-working using water grinding technique. In the past, they have traded with Yarkand".[7]

Yet another source which helped the development of trade between India and China via Central Asia was the conquest of the Sinkiang region by the armies of the Chinese emperor, Ch'ien-lung during 1756 and 1758 CE. It opened a new route for the flow of Hindustan jades to Peking via Yarkand. The Chinese ruler was very fond of Hindustan jades for their extraordinary beauty and workmanship. As regards to the refined workmanship of Indian Jade-carvers, the emperor admired their super quality and cleverness so much that he declared them superior to the Chinese jade-carvers.[8] As and when, he received a Hindustan jade-specimen, either as a gift or purchase, the emperor wrote a poem in its praise. He would further ask his court scribes to inscribe the text of the poem on the surface of that particular jade object. He thus wrote enormous amount of verses and prose which are now called "Collected poetry". So far, twenty five such inscribed jades are known, of which six such jades are found dispersed throughout the different collections of the world. The remaining nineteen appear in the jade-collection of the National Palace Museum, Taipei.[9]

The Chinese ruler, Ch'ien-lung continued to compose such commemorative verses since 1756-94 CE. In 1795, he stepped down in favour of his son, Chia-Ching who did not take much interest in Hindustan Jades. The Indian jade-trade, however, seems to have lingered on for some more time. Thus the commemorative verses Composed by the Chinese monarch, Ch'ien-lung for more than three decadès provide the best and trustworthy account of jade-trade which existed between India and China via Sinkiang. It further throws valuable light on the history and development of Indian jade-art.

As regards to the decorative motifs, like leaves, buds and flowers which cover the surface of the vessels, the emperor mentions that they are so finely carved in low relief that their polished finish left no traces of the carving process. This kind of fine and sensitive carving is so smooth that it will not catch the skin when touched. The emperor described this type of jade workmanship as "devilish.".[10] He further declared that such extraordinary workmanship far surpassed the best works of the Chinese jade-carvers in Soochow.

However, the Chinese scholar, Teng-shu ping does not agree with the above judgment of the emperor. She writes, "A characteristic feature of the poetry written by Chinese literate is its" exaggeration of certain points. She further writes, "The emperor's poems often praise the fine skill of the Hindustan jade-carvers who used water without abrasive, to carve and polish the jade. She goes on, "The Ch'ien-lung emperor's impression that water alone was used for this purpose was thus mistaken, but he mentions this idea in a total of twenty four poems which he wrote about Hindustan jades. It was apparently under this misperception that he praised the Hindustan jade-carvers as "devilishly" clever and "supernatural craftsmen".[11] We beg to disagree with the above remarks of the Chinese scholar. She was possibly unaware of the information provided in the *Agastya Samhita*, a manual on gemology which we have already discussed above in chapter 1. It contains an elaborate discussion on the tools and technology which were meant for cutting, sawing and polishing of precious gems, such as rubies, diamonds and emeralds etc., The same tools and technology could have been used for jade also with slight variations here and there. The manuscript is dated in Nepalika *Samvat* 456 (1334 CE). According to *Agastya Samhita*, the grinding wheels were cast with varying proportion of shellac and corundum. The mixture was cooled and moulded into the shape of the discs which were used for cutting, sawing and polishing hard stones, such as gems. Hence, there was no need to apply abrasive again during the cutting process. It was water alone which was used for lubrication. In this way, Indian technology was far advanced than the Chinese one.

Mughal art, right from its inception, has been eclectic. A number of Persian, Turanian, Venetian and western artisans were employed in the Mughal workshops right from the time of Akbar. This resulted in the inter-mingling of numerous influences in Indian art and architecture. For example, all early jade specimens of Jahangir are loaded with Persian art-motifs, forms of metal-ware and decorative designs. This overwhelming Persian impact was soon overcome by Indian artisans by introducing fresh organic motifs and forms drawn from Indian soil. The floral forms, motifs and designs in early Mughal jade-art first occur in Jahangir's time. A lotus bowl, made of dark-green nephrite, as per the legend inscribed, on it, was made at Mandu in 1617 CE. The full blown lotus petals are carved all around the outer surface of the wine cup. The other examples are the two identical tiny jade phials which are shaped like flower buds and are inscribed with the name of Jahangir. One of them is housed in Chhatrapati Shivaji Maharaj Vastu Sangrahalaya, Mumbai and the other is in the State Museum, Lucknow.

The introduction of flowering plants as motif and design revolutionized the subsequent Mughal decorative vision of architecture as well as the decorative art. No doubt, it was an innovative technique brought by the artisans working under Jahangir yet; this decorative device reached its perfection during Shah Jahan's period when the leaves and flowers become more naturalistic. Here, the indigenous Indian influence asserts itself and abstains totally from the Persian impact. Thus, the floral naturalism reaches its climax during Shah Jahan's reign. The most elegant and characteristic feature of the Mughal art style is the arrangements of the flowering plants in rows or in some other combination. The reappearance of acanthus leaves on the surface of Jade cups and bowls is yet another feature of Shah Jahan's period which is a western impact introduced by the Venetian artists working in the workshops of the Mughal emperor Shah Jahan. The most interesting and eye-catching decorative device of Shah Jahan's period is the curling of leaves at the extreme end and raised slightly from the surface on which it is carved. It refers to the very close observation of Nature by Indian craftsmen. No doubt, the artisans working under Aurangzeb's time continued to follow the same technique and decorative devices of Shah Jahan period. The French traveller, Bernier, who was present in Aurangzeb's court, confirms this point. Although, the artisans of Aurangzeb copied the stylistic features of Shah Jahan's period yet, they could not reach that standard.

As regards to the thin, sensuous carving, lustrous polish and organic forms of jade vessels, which were perfected during Shah Jahan period, the same continued during subsequent period also. The Chinese emperor, Ch'ien-lung greatly admired the above qualities of Indian jade. It was possibly his personal liking which boosted the jade-trade between India and China via Sinkiang. It led Indian jade-carvers to innovate new techniques, forms and decorative devices to make their products more attractive for the Chinese market. The Chinese scholar, Teng-shu ping, who has made an intensive study of the Indian jade collection in the National Palace Museum, Taipei, has noticed that the Indian jades brought to the Chinese emperor via Sinkiang during 1770 CE exhibit ever greater thinness which is not found in earlier examples of the Mughal jade specimens.

Trade with the Eastern World

The encouragement provided by the Chinese ruler, Ch'ien-lung did inspire the Indian jade-craftsmen to go beyond Indian borders and trade with the eastern world. Hence, the Indian artisans focused their trade with China via Sinkiang region. An eye witness account given by the French Traveller, Bernier, during the late seventeenth century is quite interesting in this regard. Bernier mentions about the ancient trade route which ran from Kashmir to Kashgar and China via Tibet. The Carvan merchants, who every year passed from Kashmir and reached China via Tibet had established a very brisk jade trade between India and China. They brought back with them the costly items, such as musk, rock crystal and the jade stone which had good market here in India. According to Bernier, the trade route through Great Tibet to reach China was closed by the Tibetian King since the time of Shah Jahan whose irruption into Great Tibet had offended the Tibetian king. The Tibetan king since then had interdicted the passage not only for Carvans but also had forbidden any person from Kashmir to enter his dominion.[12] This statement of Bernier would suggest that the jade trade between India and China very much existed at the time of Shah Jahan and even earlier also.

Bernier has further mentioned that the Mughal lapidaries of Aurangzeb were actively engaged in producing fancy items of jade for the royal household. He goes on, "The Jachen (jade) stone is of bluish colour, with white veins, so hard that it can only be cut with the powder of diamonds and highly esteemed at the court of the Mughals. Cups and other vessels are made of which I have some in my possession, most superbly gilt, and of very curious manufacture.[12] Bernier acted as a court physician to Aurangzeb and hence his accounts cannot be doubted.

Bernier, the physician of Aurangzeb, has specifically stated that jade as a raw material was regularly imported to India during the time of Mughal emperor, Aurangzeb and, in return, the carvan merchants must be exporting finished jade-specimens to Central Asia and China which had good market for Indian jade vessels and other miscellaneous items. We may therefore safely infer that there existed a brisk jade trade amongst India, Central

Asia and China via Tibet during the 17th-18th century CE. After the period of Shah Jahan and Aurangzeb, the Indian carvan merchants travelled to China via Sinkiang which was possibly a shorter route.

The statement of Bernier is further confirmed by the Chinese ruler, Ch'ien-lung (1736-1795 CE) in his book, *Imperial Maps of Western Region,* wherein he writes, "Hindustan is located to the south-west of Mount Patako and east of Afghanistan. Their artisans excel at jade working using water grounding technique. In the past they have traded with Yarkand". It would suggest that the trade between India and China had existed even prior to the rule of Chinese emperor, Ch'ien-lung. The Chinese emperor had also sent an imperial letter and gifts in order to encourage the trade.

The Chinese ruler, Ch'ien-lung was a great connoisseur of Indian jade-art. His commemorative verses, which he wrote in praise of Indian jade objects that were presented to him, are very useful to know the techniques and excellent workmanship which existed during late seventeenth and eighteenth centuries CE. He uses a number of metaphors and similes to describe the beauty and quality of Indian jade workmanship.

Further, the inlay of gold and silver wire and studding of precious gems to delineate floral motifs and designs became very popular with the artisans of Aurangzeb's period. The carving of jade hilts of swords and daggers shaped as heads of birds, such as peacock, parrots and wild animals, like wild goat's, horses, camels and lions etc., remained equally popular during late seventeenth and eighteenth centuries CE. There are several daggers with their hilts carved in the shape of animal's heads in the collection of Salar Jung Museum which can be dated to seventeenth and early eighteenth century CE (Pl. 26). Similarly, a number of new techniques were invented to produce novelties in their art. For example, pietra-dura and open-workmanship techniques were introduced which brought a new look to their objects. The Indian jade carvers brought out various new changes in style, form and decorative motifs in their art so as to attract the attention of their foreign buyers. For example, the inlay of one stone over the surface of the other to bring out floral design, which is popularly known as pietra-dura work, was introduced in Jahangir's architecture during seventeenth century CE. It was further revived with greater force during eighteenth century CE. There are various examples of pietra-dura work in the collection of Salar Jung Museum, Hyderabad.

A green jade book-stand (no. XLIX-19) datable to seventeenth century CE is a fine example of pietra-dura work (Pl. 27). The entire surface of the book stand is carved with the acanthus leaves and flowers which are made of white jade over the green surface. Yet another very fine example of pietra-dura work is a mirror back made of dark green jade and inlaid with a plant showing leaves and flowers made of white jade all around the surface (no. XLIX-126) (Pl. 28). Yet another decorative device, "open-work" technique was also very popular during 18th-19th century CE in India. A very finely carved mirror back of white jade, exhibiting floral plant in the centre and the border showing acanthus leaves projecting outside (no. XLIX-131) (Pl. 29). Yet another mutton fat jade lid, round in shape, is a very excellent example of the open-workmanship belonging to eighteenth century CE, which is housed in Salar Jung Museum (no. XLIX-575) (Pl. 30). Yet another decorative technique which was employed by Indian jade carvers of late eighteenth and nineteenth century had produced large number of jade wine cups, bowls and vases with their handles made to show as leaves and flowers carved in different style. A jade wine cup with its bud-shaped handles on either side is a fine example of this technique, datable to eighteenth century, is also housed in Salar Jung Museum, Hyderabad (no. XLIX-87) (Pl. 31). Another bowl made of white nephrite with small ring base and two lobed handles shown as lowering buds and the entire outer surface carved in floral motif is also housed in Salar Jung Museum, Hyderabad (no. XLIX-614) datable to late eighteenth century (Pl. 32).

Changes in Indian Jade-carving

Coming to the end of eighteenth and nineteenth centuries, a variety of changes appear in the carving of Indian Jade specimens. These changes occur in matters of form, technique and decor. The Indian jade carvers began to use ancient Chinese vessels in their design to produce their models. These new models, such as bowls, cups, vases and plates look like Chinese with features such as lobes, spouts, leaf-shaped back handle etc. They are carved with extremely thin and translucent carving. The decorative features, like lobes, spouts, leaf-shaped back handle, movable rings and chains attached to the bud-shaped lids are very common features to these new models which were meant to attract the attention of their oriental buyers.

Dish made of white jade, shaped like a flower with its petals emerging from beneath to act as the base. The two fish-shaped handles one on each side are very beautiful. Dated eighteenth century CE (no. XLIX-135) (Pl. 33).

We find such Chinese type vessels carved by Indian jade carvers in different collections of the world. A vase (no. XLIX-592) made of white jade in the collection of Salar Jung Museum Hyderabad, is a true example of these nineteenth century Chinese type Indian jade vessels. The carving is so thin and translucent that its external decor can easily be seen through inside surface. Hence it has no weight. The outer surface is covered with decoration of leaves and flower patterns in overlapping layers and extremely thin walls. The leaf-shaped handle has moveable ring and chain attached to the bud-shaped lid (Pl. 34).

Yet another example is a bowl (no. XLIX-595) again in the collection of Salar Jung Museum, Hyderabad, which is made of white jade. The extremely thin carving of the wall, high ring foot, acanthus leaf-shaped lobed handle along with a moveable ring are the prominent features of the Chinese art which were adopted by the Indian craftsmen. The acanthus leaf-shaped rear lobed handle is attached to the rim. The leaf and flower pattern is carved over the external surface. It is datable to nineteenth century CE (Pl. 35).

References

1. Robert Skelton, *The Relation between the Chinese and Indian Jade Carving Traditions*, p. 107.
2. *Ibid.*
3. Munshi Muhammad Kazim, 'Alamgir Namah', *Royal Asiatic Society*, 1868, Calcutta.
4. Robert Skeleton, *Fifth International Congress of Turkish Art*, edited by Feher, p. 797.
5. C.Y. Watt, *Poppy Blossom Bowl - Mughal and Mughal Style Jades*, p. 115.
6. Francois Bernier, *Travels in the Mughal Empire*, Translated from the French by Irving Brock, vol. II, London, 1826, p. 167.
7. Teng-Shu-Ping, *Catalogue of a Special Exhibition of Hindustan Jade in The National Palace Museum*, Taipei, 1983.
8. *Ibid.*
9. *Ibid.*
10. *Ibid.*
11. *Ibid.*
12. S.R. Sarma, "Historical Notices on Gem-Cutting in India", In: G. Kupparam and K. Kumudamani (eds.), *History of Science and Technology in India*, vol. V, 1990, Delhi, pp. 144-145.
13. Francois Bernier, *op. cit.*
14. *Ibid.*
15. C.Y. Watt, *Chinese Jades from the Collection of the Seattle Art Museum.*

Appendix 1

Agastya Samhita – Historical Notices on Gem Cutting in India*

For the early medieval period, much valuable information can be gathered from a recently published manual on gemology entitled *Agastya Samhita*. The edition is based on a single manuscript that was copied in Nepalika *Samvat* 456 (1334/35 CE) at Phanapigu (Modern Pharping) by a Maharashtrian Pandit Damodara at the instance of Prince Rauta Jivasimhadeva during the reign of Maharauta Jaitasimhadeva. This manuscript was copied from another one belonging to the merchant Jayasiha Bharoka, son of Sihanayaka of Tetava. The latter manuscript may have been copied around the end of the 13th century and the text itself may not be much older.

Besides the usual topics of the traditional gemology, the *Agastya Samhita* contains elaborate discussions on the tools and equipment of the lapidary. Since accurate descriptions – indeed even the names– of tools and techniques are rarely to be met

* Published in *History of Science and Technology in India*, G. Kuppuram and K. Kumudamani (eds.), Sundeep Prakashan, Delhi.

with in Sanskrit texts, the *Agastya Samhita* proves to be an invaluable record for the history of technology. Therefore, I shall discuss these tools in somewhat greater detail. There are 9 varieties of grinding and polishing wheels (*sana*) and 6 types of diamond drills (*vajra*).

Grinding Wheels

The first five varieties are cast with varying proportions of shellac (*laksha*) and corundum (*kuruvinda*), Crushed corundum is thoroughly mixed with molten shellac, the mixture is cooled and moulded into the shape of disks. The text prescribes the manufacturing of these grinding wheels in the following manner.

1. *Kharasana* (coarse grinding wheel) : This is cast with coarse grains of corundum mixed with a small quantity of shellac, presumably the minimum (say, about ˇof corundum) required to bind the corundum grains together.
2. *Baddhasana* : This is made with 3 parts corundum powder and 1 part shellac. The text prescribes that the corundum should be first pounded into fine powder and then strained through a cloth. The name which literally means "grinding wheel in which (corundum and shellac) are bound together "does not suggest anything about the function of this wheel.
3. *Kinasana* : This wheel is fashioned with equal parts of corundum and shellac, and is supposed to remove the granular parts (kina) from the surface of the gem.
4. *Sprstasana* : This has 2 parts corundum and 3 parts shellac and is used for making the gem very smooth. The name suggests that the gem is lightly touched with this wheel.
5. *Malasana* : This is cast with a mixture in which shellac constitutes the third part, i.e. 2 parts corundum and 1

part shellac. This is described as the remover of impurities (*mala*) on the surface of the gem.

The sequence in which the wheels are enumerated in the text does not follow the proportion of the corundum in the mixture. The correct sequence in the descending hardness of the wheel will be as follows:

Kharasana	shellac:	corundum	1 : 4 (approx.)
Baddhasana	shellac:	corundum	1:3
Malasana	shellac:	corundum	1:2
Kinasana	shellac:	corundum	1:1
Sprstasana	shellac:	corundum	1:2/3

From this gradation, it is possible to conclude that the gemstone was ground successively on all these grinding wheels. First it was ground to a rough shape on the *Kharasana*, then the shape was made more pronounced by grinding on the *Baddhasana*. In the third stage, superficial impurities were presumably ground away on the *Malasana*. The *Kinasana* is clearly meant for the next stage of the operation, viz. removing the pits, scatches and wheelmarks from the surface of the gem. This stage is called 'sanding' in modern parlance. Then the gem was lightly touched on the *Sprstasana* in order to give pre-final polish.

Polishing Wheels

For the final polish, the *Agastya Samhita* prescribes 4 types of wheels, each wheel apparently for different species of gems.

1. *Kasthsana*: This is made from the smooth timber of *Salmalia malabarica* Scott. et Enat. (Salmali). Water should be applied while polishing on this wheel.

2. *Mrcchana* : This is cast with equal parts of shellac and black earth (*krsnamrd*) and ahes of *Schrebera swietenoides* Roxb. and other trees are applied to this wheel.
3. *Tamrasana* : This is a copper wheel coated with burnt gara. On this hard gems such as ruby are polished.
4. *Diptisana* : This is made from the timber of *Calotropis gigantea* R. Br. This wheel is moistened and coated with the ashes of cow-dung.

Different types of polishing powders, mixed with water and made into paste (*vatika*) were applied to these wheels. Thus ashes of certain timbers to the wheel made of shellac and black earth, ashes of cow-dung to the one carved out of the wood of *Calotropis gigantea* R. Br., And powder of burnt gara to the copper wheel mentioned in the test. In Jaipur, garade notes today the dust from the gemstone and from the grinding wheel, which is collected and used as polishing powder. Whether the same meaning applies to our text is uncertain. It is stated that hard gems (*maharatna*) such as ruby, i.e. ruby, sapphire, emerald are polished on the copper wheel. Presumably the other wheels were used for polishing gems of lesser hardness. Today in Jaipur, copper wheels are employed for facet cut and those made of *Calotropis gigantea* R. Br. for Cabochon cut.

The text is also silent on the mechanism for rotating these nine types of grinding and polishing wheels. It is however, conceivable that they were fixed to a spindle that ran between two upright posts. And that spindle was rotated by means of a bow-like contraption. It is also likely that the cutting bench was so constructed that the wheels could be interchanged as the occasion demanded. Finally, lubrication with water is prescribed only in the case of the first polishing wheel, but this must have been done with all types of wheels, in order to cool them and also to wash off the gem dust from the cutting edge.

Mortar

In addition to these wheels, the text describes one more apparatus for grinding called *dronika.* This is a wooden mortar the inner surface of which is coated with a layer of mud to which corundum powder is applied. Gems are ground in this apparatus, and the depression of the mortar is well noted for cutting gems *em cabochon.*

Diamond Drills

The second set of tools is styled *vajras* because diamond is incorporated in them.

1. *Vajrachakra*: This is a drill (*bhrama*) to the end of which some straight pieces of diamond are affixed so as to form a wheel. The text states that this tools is employed in maniyojanakarma, i.e. operation of joining gems. One would expect rather the opposite, *manibhedana,* i.e sawing or splicing the gemstones.
2. *Vedhavajra* : Here a solid piece of diamond is cemented to the tip of the metal rod of the drill, and this tool is used for boring holes in gem beads. We know this tool already from Kalidas.
3. *Sucivajra* : This consists of a large diamond with needle sharp tip, which is attached to the drill. This tool is meant for carving various types of figurines.
4. *Lekhavajra* : Here a diamond is affixed to the end of the drill in such a way that the sharp point of the diamond is at right angles to the rod of drill. This is employed in engraving.
5. *Chedanavajra* : A diamond with notched cutting edge is attached to the drill. Perhaps this tool is used for grinding the diamond to the desired shape.

6. *Upamarajanavajra* : The text on this tool is rather obscure. Apparently a diamond with smooth surface is affixed to the drill, and this is used for polishing diamond. Lubrication with water is recommended for this tool.

Appendix 2

Khawasul Jawahara — Some Information on the History of Jade-Art of Central Asian Region*

Khawasul Jawahara is rare Persian manuscript dealing primarily with the medicinal qualities of precious and semi-precious stones. While describing the medicinal and magical qualities of Jade, the author yields some very valuable and rare information regarding the history of the art of jade, carving of Central Asian region which is of prime interest to the scholars working on the genesis of the Islamic jade art tradition. The said treatise is presently housed in the manuscript collection of the Salar Jung Museum Library at Hyderabad.

The scribe of the manuscript, Mirza Lutf Ali Baig informs us that it was copied from an earlier treatise written for the Central Asian monarch, Shah Rukh, a great patron of learning and art. As it was written for Central Asian monarch, Shah Rukh,

* Published in *The Glorious Heritage of India (In Memory of Prof. R.C. Sharma)*, S.D. Trivedi (ed.).

the information contained therein can safely be treated as true and trustworthy. Mirza Lutf Ali Baig had copied it in 1270 H from the original manuscript written by Mohammad Haji for the Turkish ruler, Shah Rukh.

The information which is of prime interest to us is about the history of the art of jade-carving in Central Asian region. The three main points which come out of the description provided therein are as follows. Firstly, it says that jade as a semi-precious stone was held in high esteem by the nobles of Khata. It was found in the areas around the regions of Kashgar and Khotan and it was in seven colours.

The second point which is of utmost importance to know the history of jade-carving in Central Asia is that it was the Kafirs living at Khata who had the mastery over the art of jade-carving. Their workmanship, both in engraving (Naqs-i-Khatai) and in delineating perfect figures, forms and motifs (Suratagiri), was of such a high standard that people got puzzled after witnessing the same. They also produced sword hilts out of jade which were prized very high, so much so that a jade sword-hilt (or belt) was sold in Khata for five thousand gold-*mohurs*. The Kafirs themselves, both men and women, took pride in processing jade objects according to their social status. Even the tradesmen, who visited Khata, gained importance by acquiring beautiful jade objects.

The third point which is equally important, says that the Turks of Mawaraunhar and Khorasan initially did not show much interest towards jade art. It was, however, from the reign of Shah Rukh, who himself collected jade that the Turks got interested in this art and subsequently they became experts and produced a good number of master craftsmen in the art of jade-carving. Gauharashad Begum, wife of Shah Rukh, got prepared a *Pusht* (back of the throne?) for her son, Baisanqar Mirza, by spending a large sum of money.

The foregoing information based on our treatise written for the Turkish ruler, Shah Rukh, is of vital interest to scholars working on the history of Islamic jade. As it is evident from the above discussion, the art of jade-carving in Central Asia took its roots from the reign period of the Turkish ruler, Shah Rukh. Prior to this, the Turks did not evince interest in this particular art though the best variety of jade, which is nephrite, comes from this region. This important piece of information contained in the manuscript, Khawasul Jawahar, further gets confirmed by the archaeological discoveries in the region. So far, not a single jade object datable prior to the rule period of Ulugh Beg, son of Shah Rukh, has come to light. The story of Ulugh Beg's capture of two large blocks of jade during his Mughalistan compaign in 1425 CE is known to scholars. One of these jade blocks is now placed on the tomb of Timur, the grandfather of Ulugh Beg.

The well-known scholar, Pinder Wilson describes this jade monolith as the earliest jade-specimen in the whole Islamic world. Where as this monolith was brought and installed at the Timur's tomb by Ulugh Beg in 1424-25 CE. It cannot be earlier to the archaic jade book stand which is dated to 607 A.H. corresponding 1209-10 CE. It is presently housed in the Salar Jung Museum, Hyderabad, India. Pinder Wilson must not have seen this rare book stand. Secondly, Pinder Wilson describes this monolith as the work of a mason and not by an expert jade carvers.

It has been so far believed that the art of jade-carving in Central Asia was first introduced by the Timurid ruler. Ulugh Beg, son of Shah Rukh and grandson of Timur. A number of jade objects inscribed with the name of Ulugh Beg are known to us. For example, a jade cup with its handle carved as a hornless dragon was presented to Ulugh Beg whose name is inscribed on the side with the title Gurgani. The cup, according to Pinder Wilson, is a product of Khotanese workmanship. Further, Ulugh

Beg is also known to have brought the jade monolith, which is placed at the burial of Timur in his mausoleum. This tombstone is engraved on the upper face with a prayer niche and a memorial of Timur's ancestry in Thulth characters.

Among the finest examples is an oval cup now in the British Museum, London. It has a handle which is carved as a dragon's head. Further, a cup with a loop handle showing a Phoenix head, presently housed in Bharat Kala Bhavan, Varanasi. It is inscribed, "Ulugh Beg, Gurgani".

A part from these small cups, a number of jade jugs have also appeared. A very beautiful jade Jug, belonging to Gulbenkian Foundation, is kept in Lisbon. It has an inscription which dedicates it to Ulugh Beg Gurgani.

The view that it was Ulugh Beg who introduced the art of jade-carving in Central Asia stands refuted by manuscript khawasul Jawahar.

According to *Khawasul Jawahara,* the art of jade-carving in Central Asia was first introduced by Gauharashad Begum, wife of Shah Rukh, got prepared a *Pusht* (back of the throne?) for her son, Baisanqar Mirza, by spending a large sum of money. This fact further gets confirmed by the form of quality of treatment, execution and adornment of jade specimens found inscribed with the name of Ulugh Beg. The type of workmanship demands greater experience and training which could not have been possible for the jade-carvers of Ulugh Beg's time, if it was the beginning of jade art. For example, the jade-jug, which is inscribed with the name of Ulugh Beg and which is presently kept in Gulbenkian Foundation, Lisbon, exhibits very advanced and sophisticated technology which could not have been possible for beginners. It is quiet likely that the jade craftsmen who worked in the workshops of Ulugh Beg were not the beginners but they must have come from the regions of Kaskem and Khotan in Central Asia which was the hub of jade-carving tradition.

Khawasul Jawahara further informs us that it was at Khata alone that the local inhabitants, so-called Kafirs in our manuscript *Khawasul Jawahara,* knew and practiced the art of jade-carving in the Sinkiang region. Who were these Kafirs? How and from where they learnt the art of jade-carving? Why they are called Kafirs by the adherents of Islam? Generally speaking, those who do not believe in Allah and those who do not follow the Quranic injunctions are called Kafirs. It would, therefore, suggest that the original inhabitants of Khata who practiced jade art in that region were non-Muslims. This is why they were known as Kafirs. A glance over the history of the Sinkiang region, particularly around Kashgar and Khotan area, would possibly help us in solving this problem.

According to Dr Lokesh Chandra, an authority on the Central Asian studies, both the Chinese and Tibetan accounts mention that the entire Sinkiang region was inhabited by Indian Buddhist missionaries right from third century BCE. In fact, the foundation of the city of Khotan was laid by the son and misters of Ashoka, the great Mauryan emperor, during third century BCE. The Chinese came in direct contact with Khotan only after the conquest of Tarim basin by Han Wu-ti (140-87 BCE). At that time, Khotan was inhabited by the Indian Buddhist missionaries who had gone and settled there to propagate their faith. We also come to know from the historical records of the Liang dynasty of China (sixth century CE) that one of the Buddhist rulers of Khotan has sent an embassy to the then Chinese ruler along with several costly presents including a figure of the Buddha "carved in foreign lands". Here the reference "carved in foreign lands" should relate to India only where the best of the Buddha statues were carved under the patronage of the rulers of the Gupta dynasty, both at Mathura and Sarnath. It was during the same period, as we know from the records of the Liang dynasty (502-557 CE), that the ruler of the Gupta dynasty had also sent a "Liu-li" spittoon as attribute gift to the Chinese Court.

The foregoing description would suggest that the whole of the Sinkiang region, including Kashgar, Khotan and Yarkand, was inhabited by the Indian Buddhist missionaries and was buzzing with the activity relating to Buddhist art and culture. A more positive and trustworthy evidence to this effect is known from the travel accounts of the Chinese traveller Hiuen-T'sang who came to India via Central Asia during seventh century CE. Hiuen-T'sang makes a specific mention about a big sea-shell shaped jade slab in pale-o-white colour, measuring 2 feet in width, depicting feet of Buddha which were 1 foot and 8 inches in breadth. The carved jade slab was kept in a monastery of Kiu-Chi (Kushe) kingdom which the Chinese traveller himself had seen. Hiuen-T'sang was an enlightened Chinese scholar who could not have made any mistake in identifying the stone as jade. It is thus, clear that the early Buddhist missionaries, who had migrated to China prior to the Christian Era, had taken the technique of carving hard stone, including jade, along with them to Central Asian region. The same was continued by the descendants of early Buddhist missionaries during the subsequent periods also.

It was around 1000 CE that Islam entered the Sinkiang region. The two main tribes, viz. Uighurs and Dzungars who followed Buddhism and who ruled over Kashgar and Khotan area were defeated. The conversion of the Uighur ruler of Kashgar to Islam by the Turks marked the death knell of Buddhism and the Buddhist culture. The Turkish ruler of Kashgar further conquered Khotan in 1106 CE. The other tribe in the Sinkiang region, Dzungars, who had escaped conversion, continued to follow Buddhism till late nineteenth century when they were conquered and ousted from Khotan by the army of Ch'ien-lung in 1756-1758 CE. Both the tribes had taken jade articles along with them. The Uighurs, who were later protected by the Chinese, offered jade bowls as presents to the Chinese ruler, Ch'ien-lung which he accepted and later on he wrote poems on them. The Dzungars, while fleeing from their homes due to the Chinese attack, has left back three big jade plates which were later submitted to Ch'ien-lung. He considered them to be very important as the Dzungars might have inherited them from their forefathers. It may not be incorrect to surmise that both the tribes of Uighurs and Dzungars, as they initially followed Buddhism and also had kept their ancestral art of jade-carving alive in Sinkiang region till nineteenth century, are the people who are called "Kafirs" in our manuscript, Khawasul Jawahar. It is quiet likely that these "Kafirs" went and worked under the Timurid rulers of Samarqand sometimes around fifteenth century CE. It was under these "Kafirs" that the Turks learned the art of jade-carving and later became experts in this particular art.

Appendix 3

Discovery of a Rare Jade Book-Stand —Jade Collection in the Salar Jung Museum*

In this context, the discovery of a Jade Quran stand "Rehl" (no.14/XLIX), in the collection of the Salar Jung Museum, Hyderabad, adds new dimensions and throws fresh light on the history of jade caving in India. This unique piece of Islamic Jade bears inscriptions on both sides in archaic characters. On the obverse, it reads "Shams-ud-din Altamash Padshah" where as the reverse side reads "San 607 Hijri", in cartouches amidst a stylized form of the 'Tree of life'. It measures H. 15.6 cm and W.10.00 cm.

The book stand in question is fashioned out of one block of Jade in architectural style of the early sultanate period. The two sheets of white jade are intersected to form a base in the

* Published in *Bi-Annual Research Journal,* Salar Jung Museum, Hyderabad.

centre for holding a book. The lower portion rests on the legs shaped as those of a throne. The intervening space between the legs is carved as a conical-shaped arch of early Sultanate architecture. The Upper rim of the stand is carved with ridges to the highest point presenting slopes on two side directions. The outside surface is decked with floral designs executed in low relief. The 'Tree of Life' motif springs out of a small vase and ends with a full blown, eight-petalled flower at the top with side branches and leaves spreading around.

The owner of the book stand, as per the inscriptions on both sides, was Altamash, a king, who ruled in 607 H, equivalent to 1209-10 CE. It is known that Shams-ud-din Altamash ascended the throne of Delhi in 607 H. The jade book stand in the Salar Jung Museum, therefore, can easily be attributed to Altamash who ruled at the beginning of thirteenth century CE. Shams-ud-din Altamash, as a ruler, was famous for his religious temperament and leanings towards Islam. During this period, the art of calligraphy had reached its highest excellence and many pocket size editions of the Holy *Quran* were written by Turks and Persian in Naskh characters. It is, therefore, logical to believe that this unique and rare gift of a sacred nature which might have been made for the new King Shams-ud-din Altamash, who ascended the throne of Delhi in 607 A.H. corresponding to 1209-1210 CE.

I am thankful to Sir Robert Skeleton for his suggestion to enquire about the following points for settling the date of the above *Quran* stand.

Firstly, the script is not the same which we find in the inscribed architectural panels of the period of Altamash. Secondly, the name of the owner of the *Quran* stand is inscribed here as Altamash and not Iltutamish. It is believed by certain scholars that the form 'Altamash' is the later rendering of the original name given by Badauni at a much later date. Thirdly, the rulers of the early Sultanate period are generally mentioned in their inscriptions as 'Sultan' and not 'Padashah'. The date of *Quran* stand can be established beyond all doubt, provided the above issues are met satisfactorily.

A careful scrutiny of the coins inscriptions and other contemporary examples of art and architectural decorations, may probably meet the above objections. So far the script of the inscription is concerned, it is engraved with archaic characters which neither represent the Naskh script found in other inscriptions of the period of Altamash, nor it is developed form of Nastaliq of Early Mughal Era. For example, the curves in the lettering are not the same parallel curves as are found in the Nastaliq script. Similarly the dots in Nastaliq writing should be square whereas they are circular in the present inscription. In fact, the characters represent the initial stages of Nastaliq script while it was in the process of evolution.

The theory that the form 'Altamash' is a later rendering of the original name of Iltutamish, does not seem to be convincing as both the forms are found inscribed on the coins issued during life time of the king (see coin number 59B in the catalogue of the coins in the Indian Museum, Calcutta by Nelson Wright 1907, Part I, Part II).

Similarly, the word 'Padashah' also occurs in a fragmentary inscription from Aligarh which belongs to the period of Altamash wherein he has been mentioned as the King of Islam (Arch. Sur. India, *Epigraphia Indica*; Arabic and Persian supplement 1966 Plate II a, p. 10). After getting satisfactory answers of all the points raised by Robert Skelton, we need no further evidence to settle the genuineness of the jade-book stand under review. It is no doubt the earliest jade specimen in the whole Islamic world.

Further, its form treatment and execution which belong to Tughlaq period of Indian history, also confirm its date mentioned in the inscription. Some splendid manuscripts in

Arabic language, which date from the second half of the thirteenth century CE, exhibits the tradition of such spray like trees motif with eight-petalled flowers (*Marg*, XXIX: 76, Pl. 6 for a similar *Quran* stand and Pl. 22 for the tree).

Further, it as a beautiful piece of jade art and the date mentioned on the both sides, and the name of its owner all go to confirm it's genuineness. It is undoubtedly earliest jade specimen in whole of the Islamic art.

Pender Wilson in his learned paper, jades from the Islamic world, "Although there is no surviving jade vessel earlier than the fifteenth century, there are a number of references in historical literature pertaining to jade working. But these are statements not entirely reliable". He again writes that, the jade monolith, probably the earliest jade-carving in the Islamic world commemorating the burial of Timur in his mausoleum is of dark green nephrite, 192 cm long, 36.75 cm wide at one end and 30cms at the other end and 30 cm high. This is almost rectangular block is engraved on the upper face with a prayer niche and a memorial of Timur's ancestry in Thulth characters. It also recounts how the stone was brought back as booty by Ulugh Beg after his defeat of the ruler of Mughalistan in 1424-1425 CE.

Pinder Wilson has also remarked that the tomb stone in treatment and execution is the work of a mason rather than that of a skilled lapidary. It was made at Samarqand by native craftsmen. It would thus suggest that a school of jade-carving was established in the city of Samarqand.

In fact, a number of jade vessels are found inscribed with the name of Ulugh Beg. However, the most impressive is the jug, presently housed in the Gulbenkian Foundation, Lisbon.

We may not agree with Pinder Wilson when he describes the tomb stone of Timur datable to 1424-1425 CE, as the earliest jade in the entire Islamic world. He is possibly unaware of the rare jade book stand which lies in the jade collection of Salar Jung Museum, Hyderabad. It is not only a superb jade piece in its form, Treatment and execution but also the earliest jade piece in the whole of the Islamic world. It is dated in 607 H corresponding to 1209-1210 CE.

Appendix 4

Jade in Early Buddhist Art of Central Asia*

The word 'jade evokes brilliant colours, hardness and translucent glossy surface, and it is for these qualities that the Chinese revered jade as the most precious of all minerals and bestowed on it heavenly and magical powers. In spite of hardness, which is 6 ½ to 6 ¾ point as per Moh's scale, and the difficulty faced in fashioning jade objects, the stone in all its varieties has been cherished and worked upon for centuries. Magnificent forms, both in pale white and dark green shades, have been carved in China, Turkestan, Persia and India.

The Jade valleys (Rudkhana-i-Yashb are centered around the regions of Kashgar, Yarkand and Khotan, popularly known as the Eastern Turkestan or Tarim basin. It is from this region that the Chinese and Indians imported jade to fashion the beautiful art-objects. The inscribed jade specimens of Indian

---

* Published in *Buddhist Art of Central Asia,* B.N. Mishra (ed.), Published by Ravindra Narayan Bajpai.

origin start appearing from the period of Jahangir. It is now proved beyond doubt that the jade workmanship of the Mughal period was largely inspired by the Central Asian art traditions. The lapidaries of Jahangir possessed a number of jade vessels, belonging to the Timurid court, which acted as prototypes to fashion the early jade specimens of Mughal India.

However, it is not definitely known as to when and how the technique of jade-carving had developed in Central Asia. The purpose of this paper will be to discuss the origin of the art of jade-carving in Central Asia, which according to some well established historical sources, could be attributed to the early Indian Buddhist missionaries who had immigrated to Central Asia during the early centuries of the Christian Era.

It will not be out of context to mention here that the Tarim basin, lying on the ancient Silk Route travelled from China to the West Asian countries. The Indian tradesmen joined it through the northern route (*uttarapatha*) which took an upward direction from Mathura and opened on the Silk Route. It paved the way for a regular commercial intercourse between India and Central Asian region.

The Chinese traveller, Hiuen-T'sang, who came to India during the mid seventh century, mentions the white jade as a commodity for regular commercial transaction in India. This proves that the jade was known in India during seventh century CE. The Chinese traveller further makes mention of a big sea-shell shaped jade slab marked with the foot prints of Buddha which was kept in the monastery of Kiu-Chi (Kushe) kingdom. There is no doubt that the references speaks about a carved pale white jade slab, measuring about 2 feet (61 cm) in width and depicting the feet of the Buddha (*Buddhapadas*) which were 1 foot and 8 inches (50.50 cm) in breadth. Thus, it is for the first time that we come across a reference to the craft of jade-carving in Central Asia. It is need not be over emphasized that the Indian

Buddhist and Brahmanical colonies were established in Tarim basin in Central Asia even much earlier to the period of Hiuen-T'sang. The whole region form the western end of China to Afghanistan and Persia was replete with Buddhist *viharas* and Hindu temples, enshrining idols of divinity of both the sects. The recent archaeological researches in the region have yielded valuable inscriptional evidence and other material to show that the Sanskrit the Brahmi script, the idols of Hindu and Buddhist gods and goddesses along with numerous arts and crafts of India were introduced in the Tarim basin by the early Buddhist and Hindu missionaries. It is, therefore, not difficult to presume that the Indian lapidaries had also gone to Central Asian regions to carve the various precious and semi-precious stones such as the *lapis lazuli* and crystal, which were used in rituals as the seven precious jewels if Buddhism. Once the Indian missionaries knew the technique of carving crystal a material harder than jade, they did not find it difficult to use the new material, jade, which was easily available there, for the service of the Samgha.

In this connection, an interesting reference is found in the Annals of Liang dynasty (502-56 CE) which record that a Khotanese mission, most probably the Indian Buddhist missionaries who had gone and settled there, went to China to seek royal favour during the rule of the Liang dynasty.

Amongst the rich and valuable presents, which the Khotanese embassies brought, contained the figure - vases in glass and a jade-statue of the Buddha which was carved in foreign lands. Obviously the connotation "foreign lands" here means no other country but India wherefrom the Buddhist missionaries had originally immigrated to Khata at the beginning of the Christian Era. The Indian Buddhist missionaries rightly preferred the statue of the Buddha to be carved in Jade as jade was the most revered commodity amongst the Chinese right from the prehistoric times.

Another very important evidence in this connection although of a later date, it is met in *Khawasul Jawahara,* a treatise on gemology which was composed during the rule of Shah Rukh and later copied from the earlier text in 1270 Hijri (1854 CE) by Mirza Lutf Ali at Hyderabad in Deccan. It refers to the craft of jade-carving which was practiced by the non-Muslim natives of Khata in Central Asia. It further mentions that the people of Turkey, Mawaraunhar and Khorasan learnt this craft from the non-Muslims during the reign of Shah Rukh. It goes on adding that Gauharshad Begum, the wife of Shah Rukh, got prepared a push (seat) of jade for her son, Baisanqar Mirza, at the cost of a handsome amount. A critical analysis of the aforesaid account would suggest the following points. Firstly, the craft of jade-carving in Central Asia was in the hands of non-Muslim craftsmen during the reign period of Shah Rukh. The jade as a medium of Islamic art, was favoured not earlier than the reign of Shah Rukh. With the result, the Muslim craftsmen of Turkey and Persia learnt the technique of jade-carving from the non-Muslim residents of Khata.

The historicity of genuineness of the above account is further confirmed by the fact that the so far known earliest Islamic jades of Central Asia are inscribed with the name of Ulugh Beg, the son of Shah Rukh. Hence the tradition of Islamic carving in Central Asia seems to have started during the reign of Shah Rukh only. However, it is during the reign of Ulugh Beg that the craft got extra impetus and popularity. The Indian Mughals, particularly Jahangir had acquired a number of jade vessels belonging to Ulugh Beg. The Mughal lapidaries of Jahangir period drew inspiration from the Persian Timurid jade prototypes to fashion excellent specimens of Mughals jades in India.

However, the basic question which remains to be answered, is the identity of the so called non-Muslim craftsmen of Khata, who introduced the craft of jade-carving in whole Islamic world.

Obviously, these non-Muslim artists of Khata could not have been Chinese, as the early specimens of Islamic jade of Central Asia do not bear the slightest resemblance to the early specimens of Chinese jades.

It is thus evident that the non-Muslim native craftsmen of Khata were undoubtedly the Indian Buddhist missionaries who had migrated and settled there with a view to propagate their faith earlier to the advent of Islam in Central Asia. The Indian Buddhist must have carried along with them the required expertise and the tools to carve the harder stones such as crystal which were used in the service of *Samgha.* It would have been very easy for the Buddhist missionaries to carve jade which was an indigenous product and also softener than crystal to fashion objects for their worship. It is thus clear that the Indian Buddhist missionaries had introduced the art of jade-carving in Central Asia at the first instance. Later the adherents of Islam, who are attracted by the medicinal and magical qualities of jade not only learnt this art from the native Buddhists but improved and modified it to produce beautiful house hold vessels and other fancy items for the use of the Muslim nobility. It was during the period of Jahangir that the Central Asian art of jade-carving came in a modified form and inspired the Mughal craftsmen to fashion exquisite wine cups, sword handles, archery rings, mirror backs and *Huqqa* mohnals, etc. for the royalty. The wheel had completed the circle and the art which had once gone from India to Central Asia came back in much improved and modified form to enrich the beauty and splendor of the Mughal court.

Appendix 5

Personality of Jahangir as known through his Jade Wine Cups*

Jade as semi-precious stone has been extensively used during the Mughal Era of Indian history to fashion exquisite objects of art, particularly objects of utilitarian value. The translucent and glossy surface of Jade when inlaid with gold and studded with costly jewels, like diamonds, rubies and emeralds to delineate floral motifs and designs must have had a very pleasing effect and added to the beauty and splendor of the Mughal court. Moreover, the reputation of Jade as 'Pa-zahar' or 'antidote to poison' was possibly instrumental in the production of such large quantity of Jade wine-cups. Jade was thus considered to be the best safeguard against poisoning which was a common phenomenon with the court intrigues of the Mughal Era. Besides, Jade was equally famous for its inherent medicinal quality to act as a cure against over-intoxication. Hawkins, an English sea-

* Published in *Kala,* The Journal of Indian Art History Congress, Maruthi Nandan Tiwari and Kamal Giri (eds.).

captain who visited Agra in 1609 mentions about the quality and large variety of Jahangir's Jade wine cups of drinking cups five hundred, fifty very riche, that is to say, made of one piece of ballace ruby, and also of emeralds, of *eshim* (jade), of Turkish stone and of other sorts of stones.

The Mughal emperor Jahangir was greatly fond of alcoholic drinks, such as opium and wine. His over indulgence in opium and alcohol, which he himself admits in his memoirs, *Tuzuk-i-Jahangiri*, must have been responsible for such a large quantity of costly wine cups in his court. The most characteristic feature of Jahangiri Jade wine cups is their inscriptional evidence which throws enough light on the colourful personality of the emperor.

The vast empire with abounding fiscal resources and the unrivalled political authority probably prompted Jahangir to equate himself with the legendary rulers of the Islamic world, such as Sulaiman and Jamsheed. The former is said to possess a magical ring which bestowed on him the power of knowing the past, present and future. The latter could see the events happening anywhere in the world through the reflections in his own drinking cup. The inscription found on one of the Jahangir's wine cups, dated in Hijra year equivalent to 1613 CE reads, 'This is the cup of sap (of life) nourisher of soul, of king Jahangir, (son) of Akbar, who can see from its shadow the dome of heaven. It is the world displaying cup (i.e. Jamsheed's cup showing the events) on the face of the Earth. Even the title *Nur-al-Din Jahangir,* which he had adopted just after his occupying the Mughal throne in 1605, literally means the 'Light of the Faith, conqueror of the world'. The first Jade specimen attributed to Jahangir is an archer's ring, made of pale white jade and inscribed with the title 'Shah Salim' and datable to Akbar's period. The very title would suggest that the ring in question was made when Jahangir was only an heir – apparent and had not ascended the throne. In other word, it is datable to Akbar's period.

The second specimen is an inscribed pale-green jade wine cup, presently housed in Brooklyn Museum, USA. It is possibly the first dated Jade wine cup produced by the royal lapidaries for the emperor Jahangir. It was fashioned in the 2nd regnal year of Jahangir, i.e. 1607-08 CE. An inscription reads thus, 'The form of the cup attained completion in 1016 A.H. the central inscription in Suls character and in Tughra form reads, 'By command of His Majesty. The great Khaqan, Lord of the kings of the world, Manifestor of Divine Favours in the offices of the caliphate and Kingship, the Sun in the Firmament of world sovereignty, the Moon in the sky of Justice and Felicity, Abul Muzaffar, son of king Akbar, Nur-al-Din Muhammad Jahangir, the emperor, the warrior of the Faith. The Persian verses in cartouches, eulogizing the cup and the red wine, are inscribed throughout its upper surface.

Yet another inscribed wine cup of Jahangir, made of dark green nephrite, is presently housed in Victoria and Albert Museum, London. It is dated in the year 1022 A.H., equivalent to 1613-14 CE. A Persian verse in four cartouches around the rim reads, 'From king Jahangir, the world found order. By the ray of his justice, the age was illuminated. From the reflection of red wine, may this cup of jade be always like ruby.

The other two inscribed jade wine cups are in the Bharat Kala Bhavan, Varanasi. Inscriptions on both these cups mention that they were made during the twelfth regnal year of Jahangir son of Akbar, in 1206 A.H., i.e. 1617 CE. However, the additional information furnished here is the provenance, Mandu where the cups got fashioned. The first cup, made of dark green jade is shaped like a full-blown lotus with petals carved on the outer surface in low relief. The Persian inscription in gold is written in gold Nastaliq over carved lotus petals. It reads, The special Jade cup, which is antidote to poison (Pa-zahar) was made for Jahangir son of Akbar, at Mandu in 1206 A.H., i.e. 1617 CE. The other wine cup, also dated in 1206 A.H., i.e. 1617 CE and bearing the place name 'Mandu is fashioned in typical Chinese style of carving. Yet the workmanship is coarse as compared to other Chinese vessels. The presence of a lotus flower at bottom would further suggest its Indian origin.

The place name 'Mandu' the place of origin, the cup and date 1617 CE as found inscribed on both these Jade wine cups, are suggestive of a significant historical event. It was at Mandu that the emperor Jahangir celebrated his 45th birthday in 1617 CE with great pomp and pageantry where a large number of Mughal nobles and other high dignitaries had participated. According to 'Tuzuk-i-Jahangiri, the lapidaries of Mandu had been famous for carving crystal which is harder stone than jade. Hence the artisans of Mandu had the technology to carve Jade without any difficulty. It is quite likely that the two Jade wine cups in question were carved in the royal lapidaries to be presented to the emperor on the very auspicious occasion.

The foregoing remarks based on the legends inscribed on the Jade wine cups of Jahangir throw a welcome light on the colourful personality of the Mughal emperor. The inner urge of the emperor to be recognized as universal legendary hero of the Islamic world must have prompted him to adopt very high sounding titles which later on got inscribed on his jade wine cups. Further, his innate love for Timurid and Safavid cultural traits and norms must have augmented his ambition to emulate Persian Kings in adopting high sounding title and projecting himself as the legendary hero among the rulers of the Muslim world.

Jahangir's ardent love for Persian cultural norms and traditions had left an abiding impact on his personality. The Iranian theory of kingship which eulogized Persian rulers as personification of solar light must have inspired Jahangir to adopt the title 'Nur-al-Din Jahangir' which means 'Light of Faith, conqueror of the world'. Even in the legends found inscribed on his Jade wine cups the same concept is emphasized again by using such phrases, 'The sun in the Firmament of world sovereignty' (Jade wine cup dated 1607-08) and 'By the ray of his justice the age was illuminated' (Jade wine cup dated 1613-14), etc.

Jahangir appears to have been greatly impressed by the Iranian symbolism of light opposing darkness. In one of his allegorical paintings, Jahangir is shown shooting arrows against a black demon symbolizing darkness. A large hallow around his head is a mark of divinity. The two heavenly angels, hovering in the sky, hold a crown over his head. The third one, standing below, offers him arrows. The emperor is standing on the globe which is suggestive of his vast dominions or universal sovereignty. The figures of a lamb and a lion are shown seated face to face on the globe which would signify peace. A large fish is holding the globe on its back, an old Islamic belief. A man lying on the fish, holds a book in his hands. Some scholars have identified him as Manu, the Hindu law giver. The artist has not forgotten to emphasise the imperial justice in the painting. Jahangir's Justice is symbolized by the chain of bells alternating with Yak tails tied to a post set on a plinth. In order to emulate the legendary ruler Anushirwan, Jahangir has ordered that these bells should be suspended from his palace above the walls of Agra for so that the petitioners could gain his attention at any time. This visual depiction very well confirms the written evidence which is found inscribed on the Jade wine cups of the emperor. In the above depiction, art goes beyond forms, motifs, line and colours. It provides a deeper meaning to highlight the personality of its owner.

Bibliography

Beal, S. (1884) *Siyu-Ki : Buddhist Records of the Western World*, vol. 1.

Bernier, Francois (1826) *Travels in the Mughal Empire*, Translated from the French by Irving Brock, vol. II, London.

Birdwood, George C.M. (1880) *The Industrial Arts of India*, London.

Chandra, Lokesh (1999-2000) 'The Cultural Linkage of India', *Citi Vithika*, 5 (142).

Chandra, Moti (1939) 'The Art of Cutting Hard Stoneware in Ancient and Modern India', *Journal of the Gujarat Research Society*, 1 (4), Bombay.

Fazl, Abul (1904) *The Akbar Nama*, translated by H. Beveridge.

Foster, W. (1921) *Early Travels in India*, Oxford.

Fryer, John (1985) A New Account of East India and Persia in Eight Letters, being nine years travels, begun 1672 and finished 1681 (London 1698), reprint, Delhi.

Gangoli, O.C. (1973) *Andhra Sculpture*, The Government of Andhra Pradesh, Hyderabad.

George, B. Parks (1927) *The Travels of Marco Polo*, New York.

Gravely, F.H. and Sivaramamurti, C (1939) *Guide to Archaeological Galleries*, Government Museum, Madras.

Habib, Irfan (1978-79) 'Technology and Barriers to Social Change in Mughal India', *Indian Historical Review*, vol.1-2.

Hansford, S.H. (1968) *Chinese Carved Jades*, London.

Irwin, John (1968) 'Mughal Jades', *The Times of India Annual*, Bombay.

Kazim, Munshi Muhammad (1868) 'Alamgir Namah', *Royal Asiatic Society*, Calcutta.

Markel, Stephen (1992) 'Inception and Maturation in Mughal Jades', *Marg: A Magazine of the Arts*, 44 (2).

Melikian-Chirvani, A.S. (1999) 'Sa ida-ye Gilani and The Iranian Style Jades of Hindustan', *Bulletin of the Asia Institute*, New Series, vol.13.

Mittal, Jagdish (1986) 'Indian Painters as Designers of Decorative Art Objects in the Mughal Period', In: M.L. Nigam (ed.), *Decorative Arts of India.*

Morley, Grace (1976) 'On Applied Arts of India in Bharat Kala Bhavan', *Chhavi*, Golden Jubilee Volume.

Nigam, M.L. 'Khawasul Jawahara - Some Information on the History of Jade-Art of Central Asian Regions', In: S.D. Trivedi (ed.), *The Glorious Heritage of India.*

Nigam, M.L. (1976-77) 'A Rare Jade Book-Stand of Sultanate Period', *Salar Jung Museum Bi-Annual Research Journal*, vol. IX and X.

Nigam, M.L. (1978) 'Souvenirs from Indian Jade', In: Mulk Raj Anand (ed.) *Glimpses of Wonder and Beauty: Indian Heritage*, Marg, 31 (2).

Nigam, M.L. (1983) 'The Mughal Jades of India', In: Karl Khandalavala and Saryu Doshi (eds.) *An Age of Splendour: Islamic Art in India*, Marg, Bombay.

Nigam, M.L. (2003) 'Early Indian Buddhist Contribution to the Jade-art of Central Asia', *Cultural Interface of India with Asia,*

International Seminar at National Museum Institute, New Delhi.

Nigam, M.L. (2004) 'Fresh Light on the History of Indian Jade-Carving', *Kala*, vol. IX.

Nott, S.C. (1936) *Chinese Jade throughout the Ages*, London.

Palmer, J.P. (1967) *Jade*, Spring Art Books, London.

Pinder-Wilson, R.H. (1960) 'An Inscribed Jade cup from Samarqand', *British Museum Quarterly*, 23 (1).

Pinder-Wilson, R.H. (1963) 'A Persian Jade Cup', *British Museum Quarterly*, 26 (1-2).

Rodgers, A. (tr.) (1909-14) *Tuzuk-i-Jahangiri*, New series, London.

Sarma, S.R. (1990) 'Historical Notices on Gem-cutting in India', In: G. Kuppuram and K. Kumudamani (eds.), *History of Science and Technology in India*, vol. V, Delhi.

Shu-Ping, Teng (1988) *Catalogue of Special Exhibition of Hindustan Jade in the National Palace Museum*, Taipei.

Skelton, Robert (1962) 'Jades Moghols', L'oeil, no. 96, Paris.

Skelton, Robert (1966) 'The Shah Jahan Cup', *Victoria and Albert Museum Bulletin*, 2 (3).

Skelton, Robert (1972) 'The Relations between the Chinese and Indian Jade Carving Traditions', In: William Watson (ed.), *The Westward Influence of the Chinese Arts from the 14th to the 18th Century*, Colloquies on Art and Archaeology in Asia, no. 3, University of London.

Skelton, Robert (1982) *The Indian Heritage Court life and Arts under Mughal Rule.*

INDEX

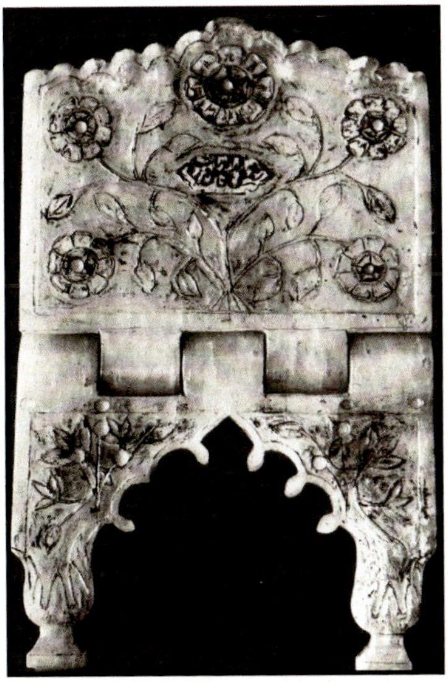

Pl. 1. An inscribed jade book-stand with the name of it's owner, Shams-ud-din Altamish *Padshah*, 607 A.H. (1209-10 CE)

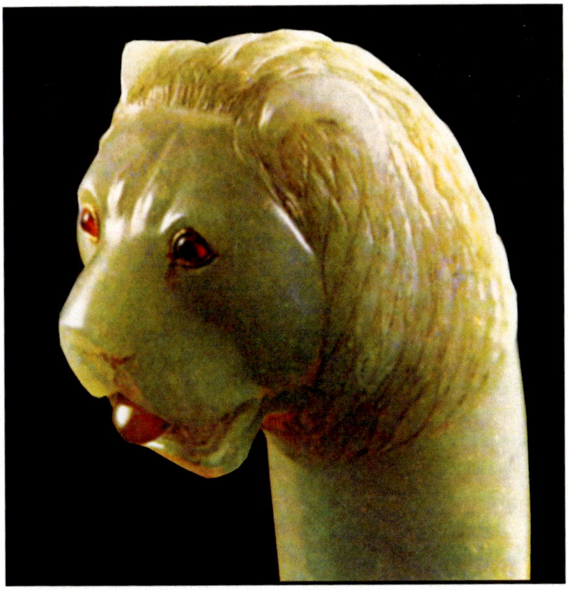

Pl. 2. A dagger shaped as lion's head and inscribed in gold letters with the name of its maker "Amal-i-Saleh", 1011 A.H. (1602 CE)

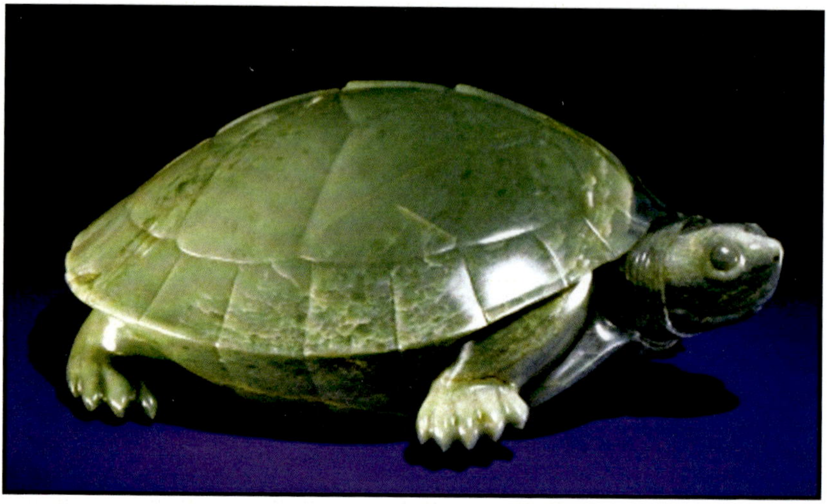

Pl. 3. A life-size tortoise, 1556-1605 CE

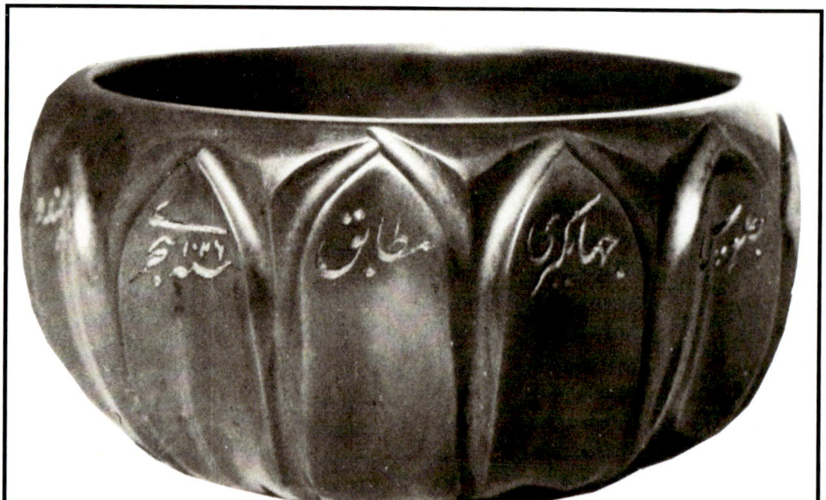

Pl. 4. Lotus cup carved in the shape of full-blown lotus flower, inscribed with name of Jahangir and the place name Mandu, 1617 CE

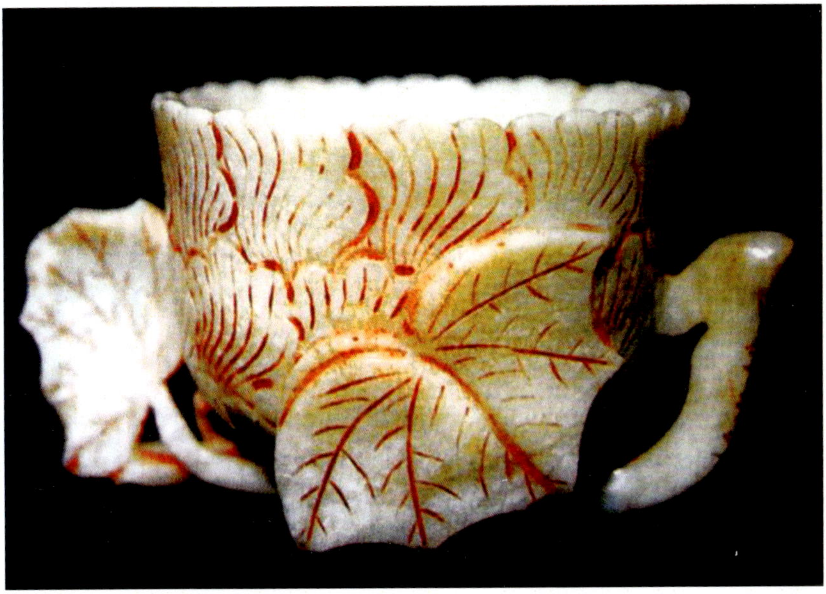

Pl. 5. Jade wine cup, inscribed with name of Jahangir and the place name Mandu, 1617 CE

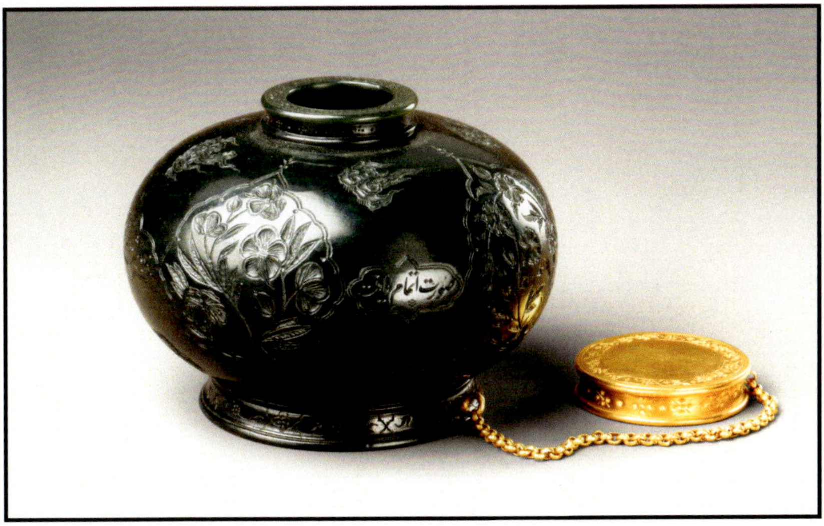

Pl. 6. Inkpot carved with dark green nephrite, inscribed with name of Jahangir, 1028 A.H. (1719 CE)

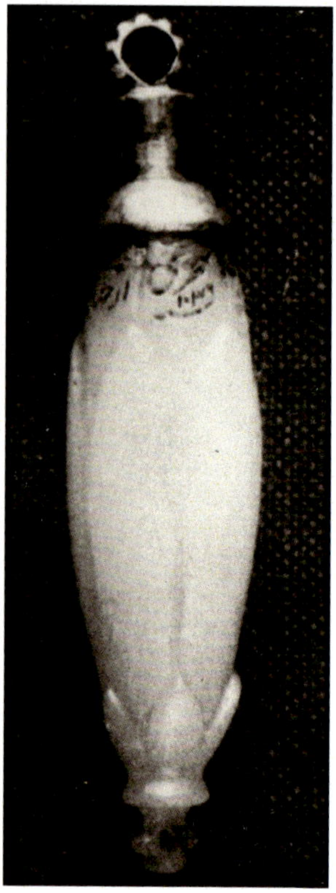

Pl. 7. A tiny jade phial of white jade, with silver mounts, inscribed on the top, giving the name of Jahangir, 1626-27 CE

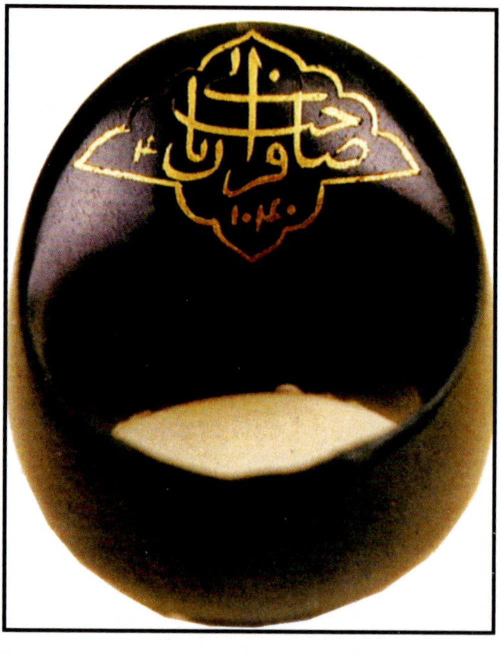

Pl. 8. Thumb ring made of dark green nephrite, inscribed with Sahib-e-Qiran-i-Sani" the title of Shah Jahan, 1040 A.H. (1631 CE)

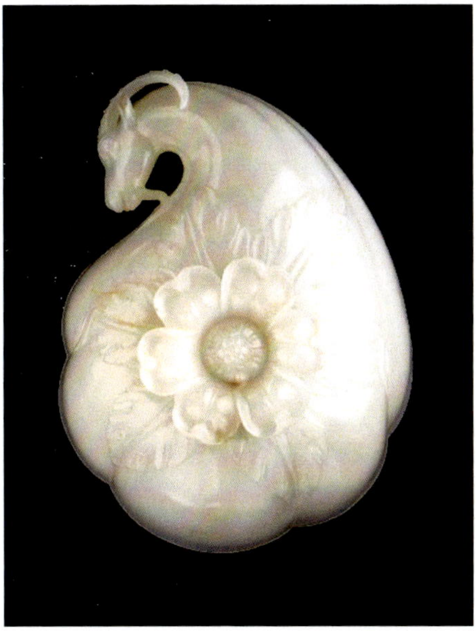

Pl. 9. Wine cup made of milky white jade, inscribed with the title of Shah Jahan, 1067 A.H. (1657 CE)

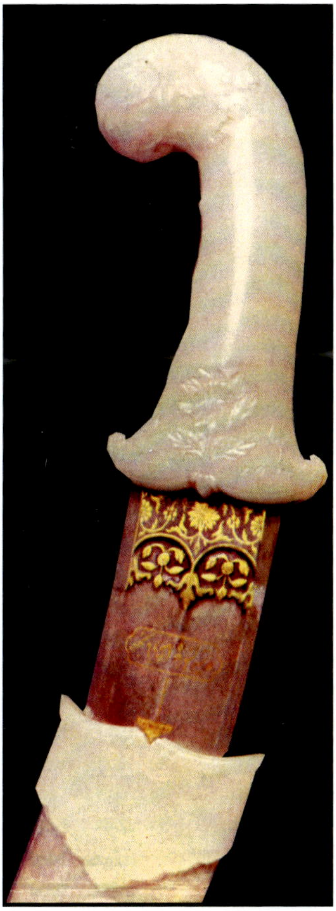

Pl. 10. Dagger with its jade hilt made of white jade, inscribed with the name Alamgir, 1072 A.H. (1663 CE)

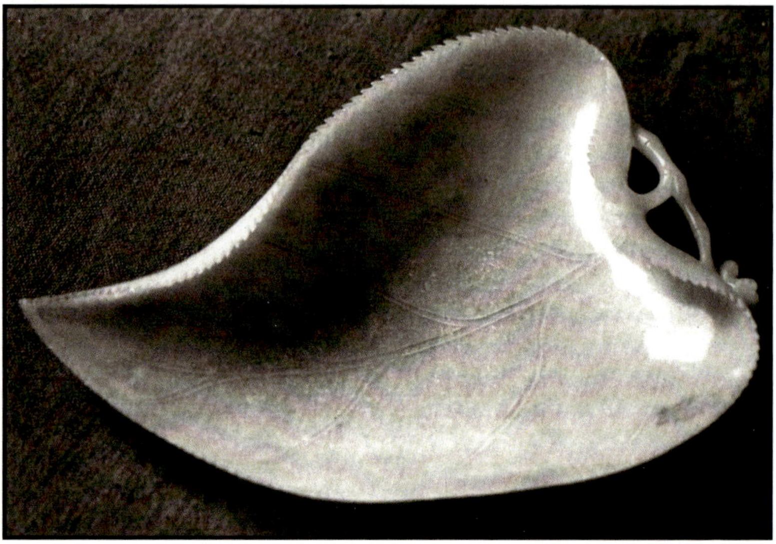

Pl. 11. Wine cup with extremely thin carving, shaped as peepal leaf, eighteenth century CE

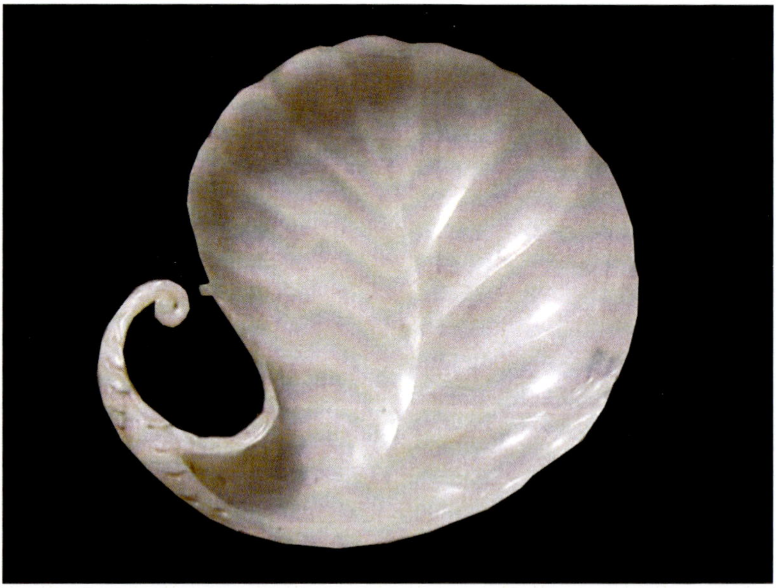

Pl. 12. A very beautiful, thinly carved jade wine cup made of white jade, Shah Jahan period

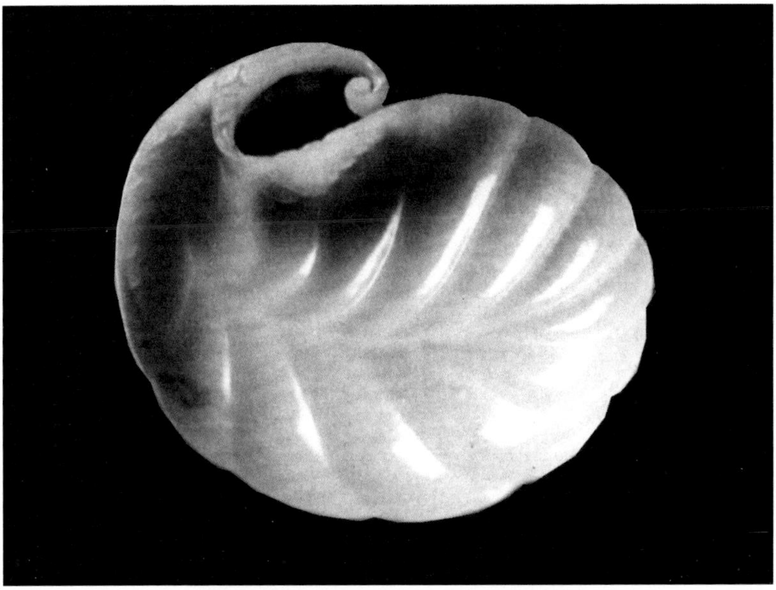

Pl. 13. An identical wine cup made of white jade, seventeenth century CE

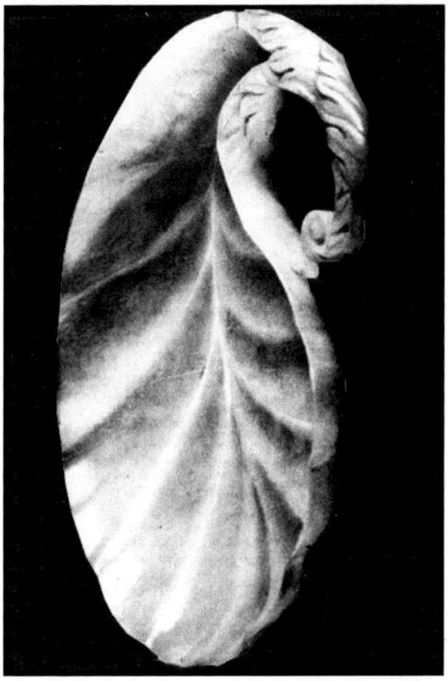

Pl. 14. Leaf-shaped wine cup made of white jade, seventeenth century CE

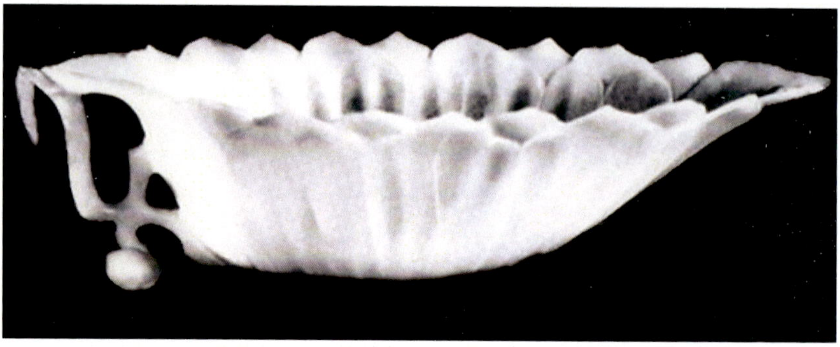

Pl. 15. Leaf-shaped jade cup made of white jade, seventeenth century CE

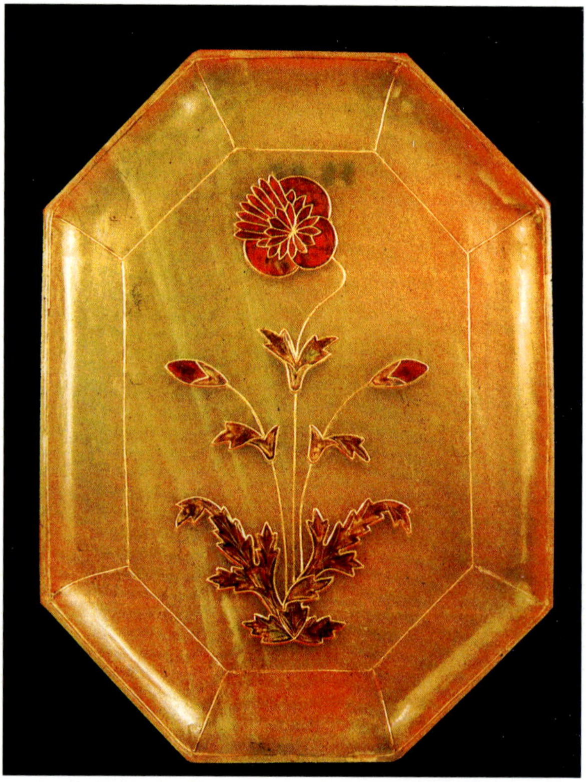

Pl. 16. A beautiful jade plate, 1627-1658 CE

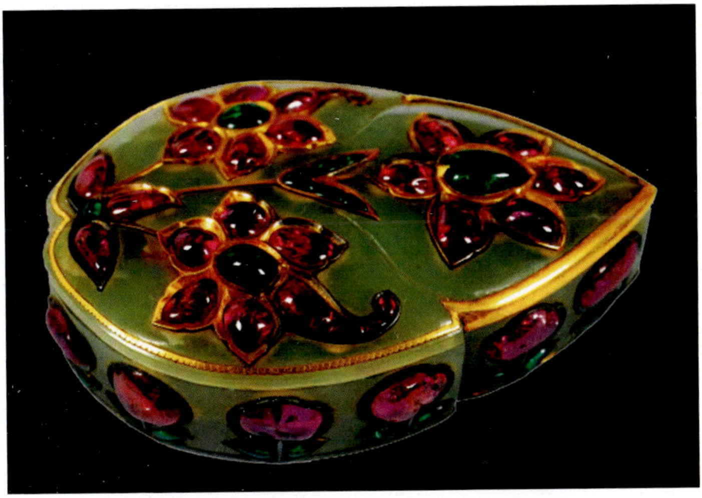

Pl. 17. Leaf-shaped jade spice box studded with precious stones, seventeenth century CE

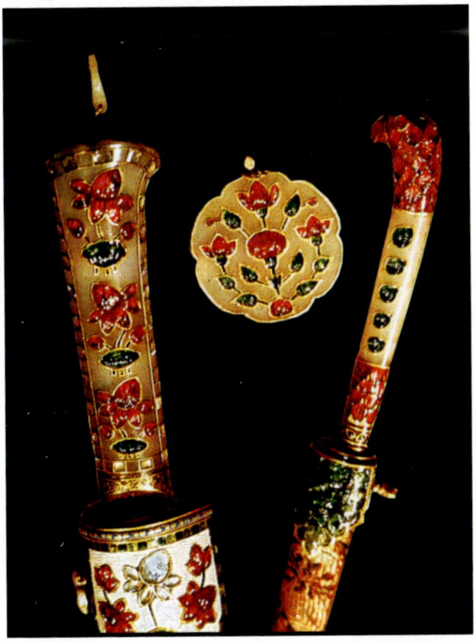

Pl. 18. Dagger with butt-shaped hilt, carved in white jade, seventeenth century CE, and Pl. 19. Fruit knife with its hilt made of white jade shaped like the head of a parrot, seventeenth century CE

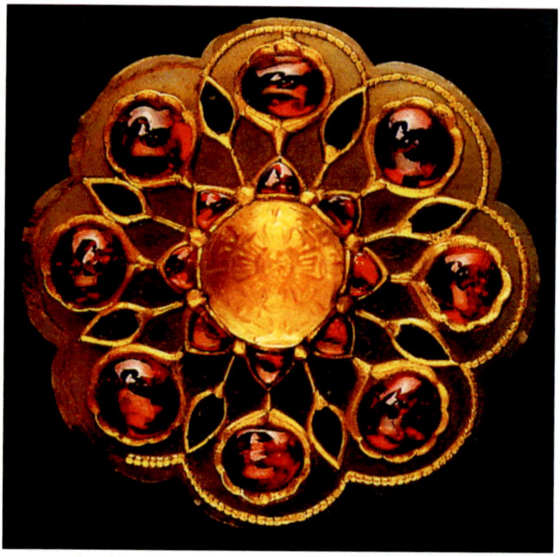

Pl. 20. Jade pendent with gold inlay, seventeenth century CE

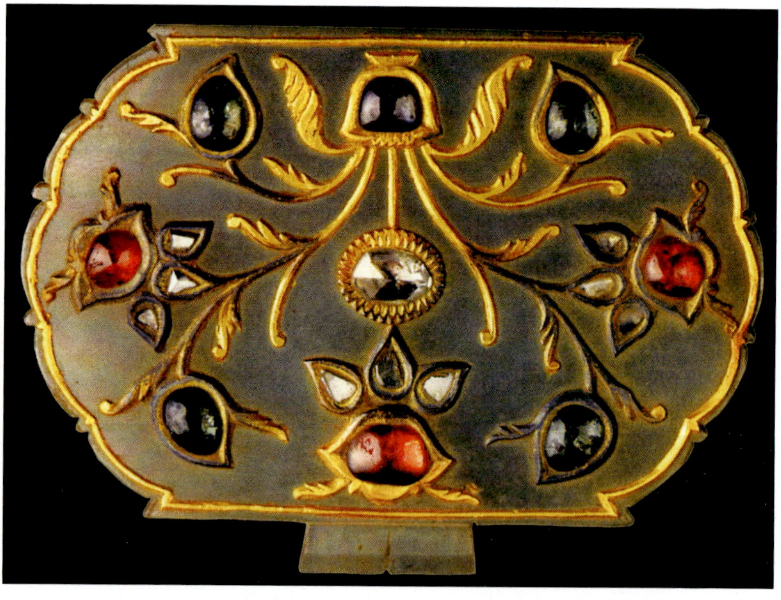

Pl. 21. Pendant made of jade with gold inlay, made of red rubies the vase is of blue Sapphire, eighteenth century CE

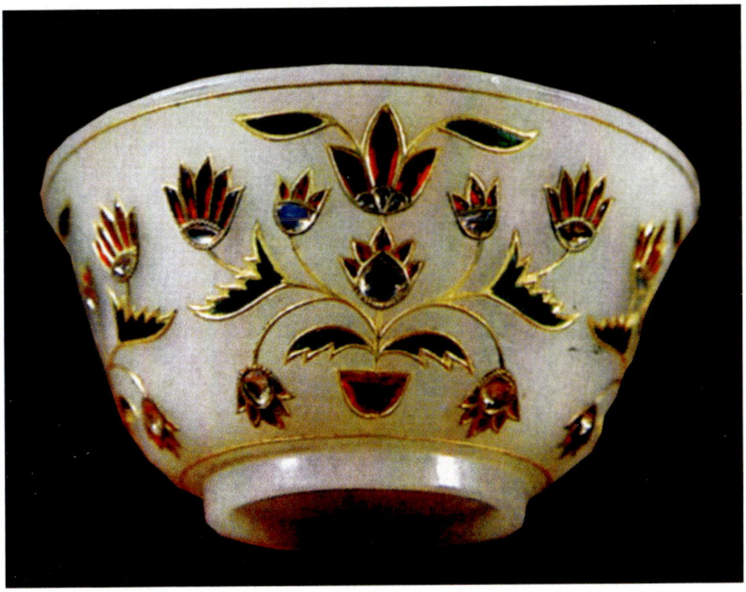

Pl. 22. Jade bowl inlaid with gems

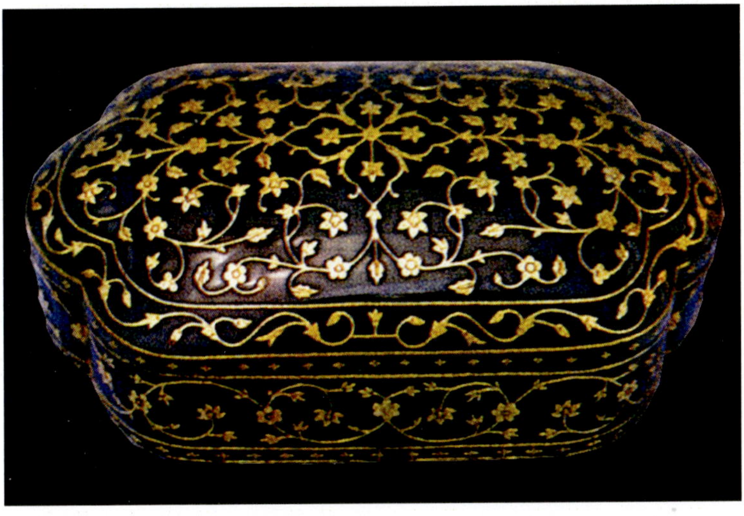

Pl. 23. Dark green jade-box inlaid in gold, eighteenth century CE

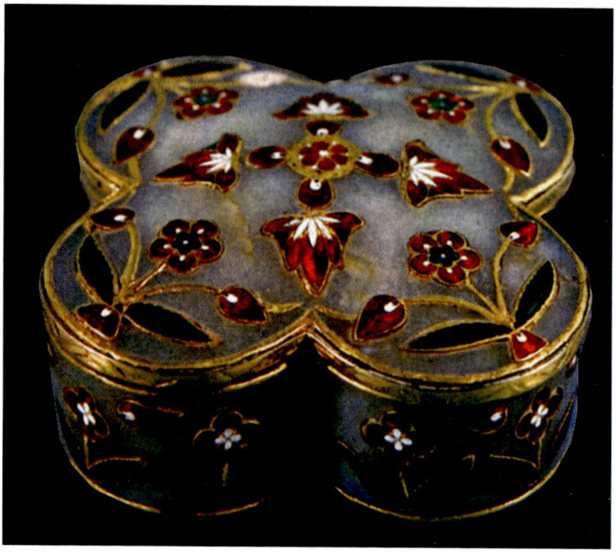

Pl. 24. Jade-box decorated with beautiful enamelling workmanship, eighteenth century CE

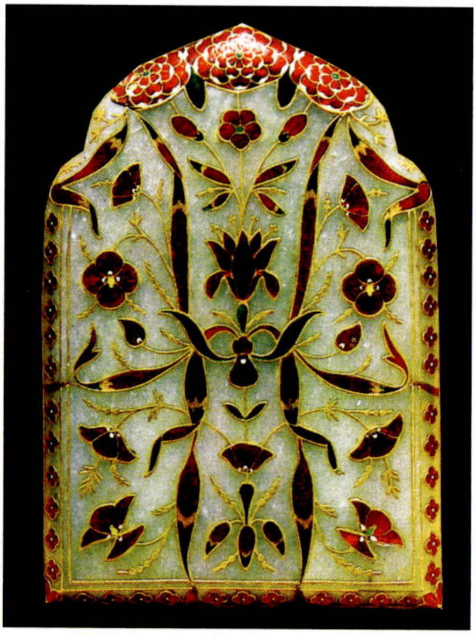

Pl. 25. Jade mirror back decorated with beautiful enamelling workmanship, late seventeenth century CE

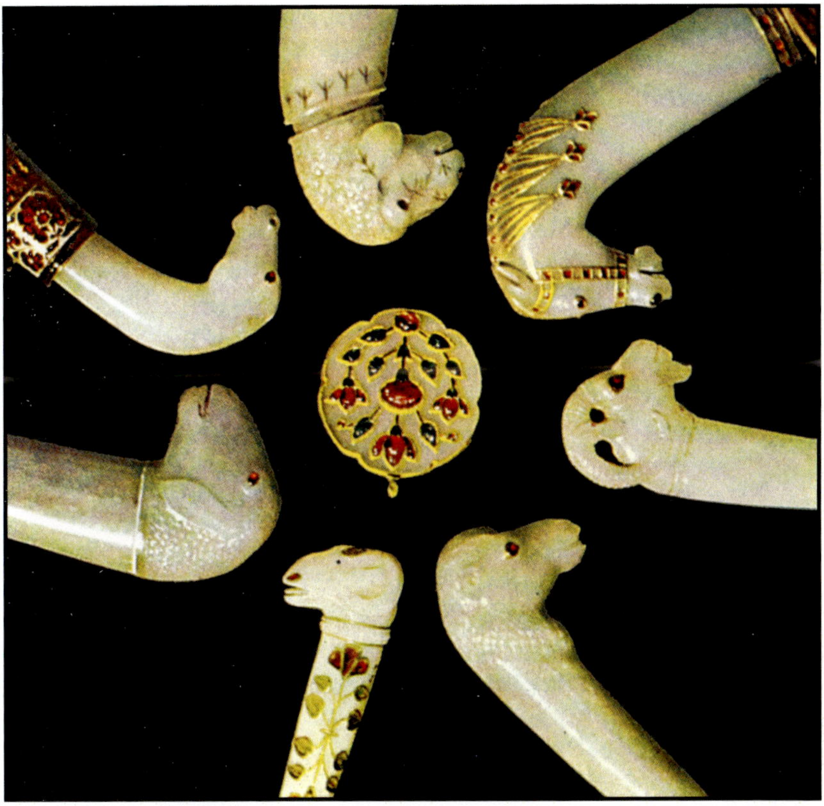

Pl. 26. Daggers with their jade hilts shaped as heads of birds and animals, 17th-18th century CE

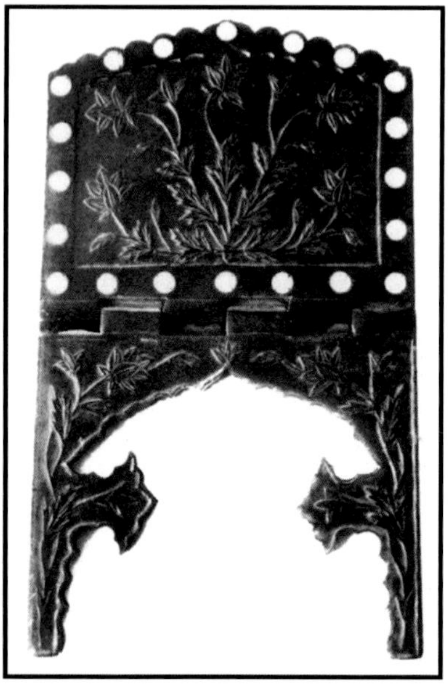

Pl. 27. Green book-stand, made from pietra-dura technique, seventeenth century CE

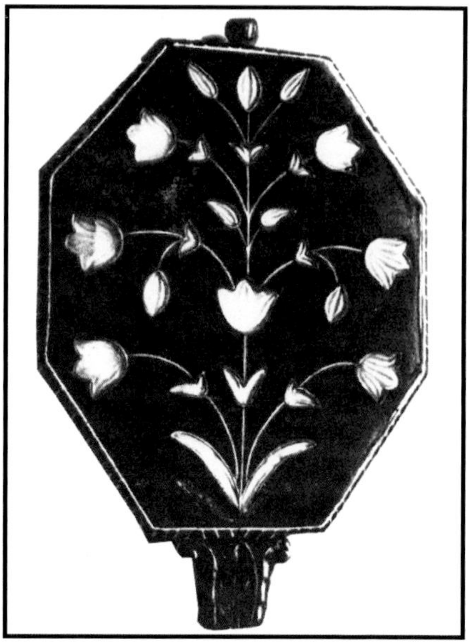

Pl. 28. Mirror back of dark green nephrite, a good example of pietra-dura technique, eighteenth century CE

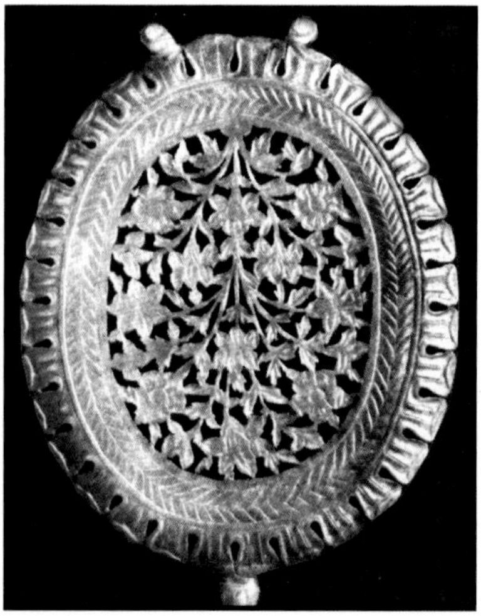

Pl. 29. Mirror back made of white jade, carved with open workmanship device, seventeenth century CE

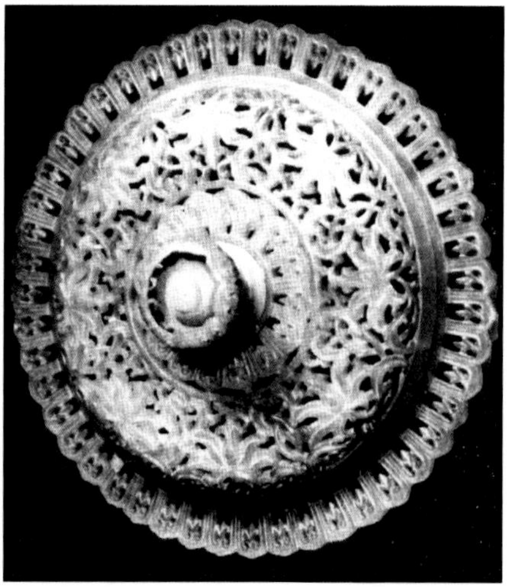

Pl. 30. Lid made of purely white jade, carved with open workmanship technique, seventeenth century CE

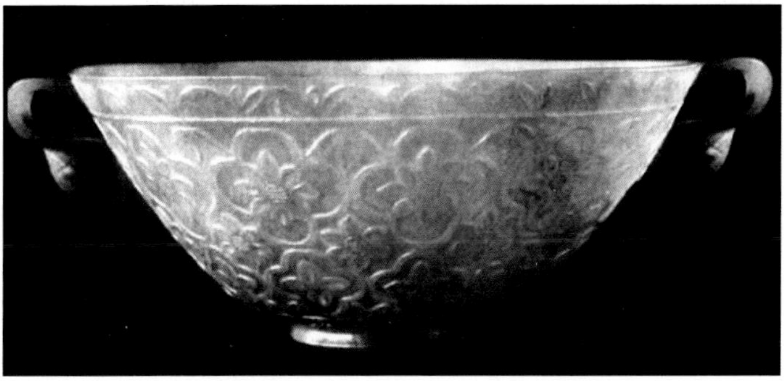

Pl. 31. Wine cup made of white jade, carved with open workmanship, late eighteenth century CE

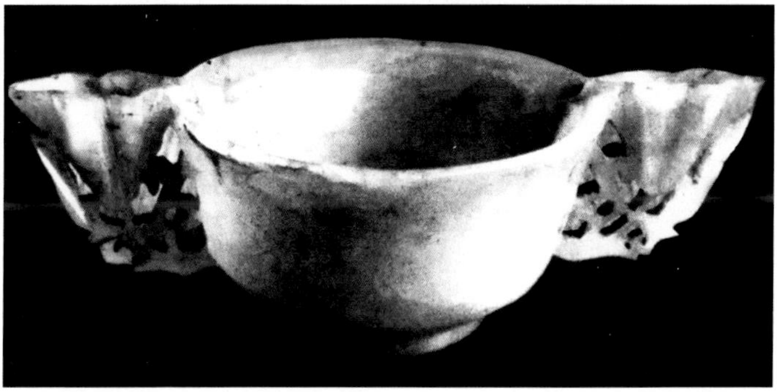

Pl. 32. Bowl made of white nephrite with small ring, late eighteenth century CE

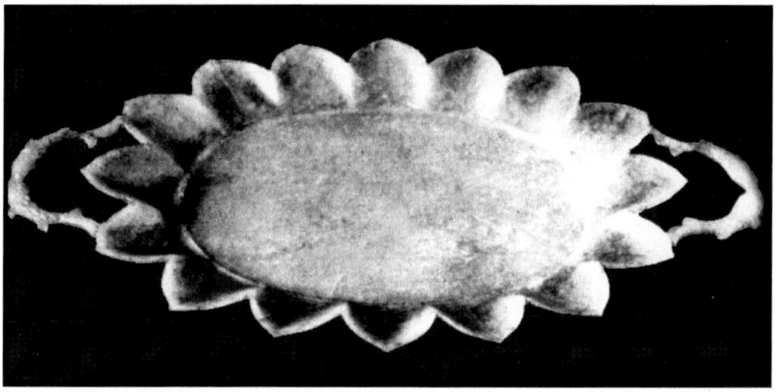

Pl. 33. Dish made of white jade, shaped like a flower, eighteenth century CE

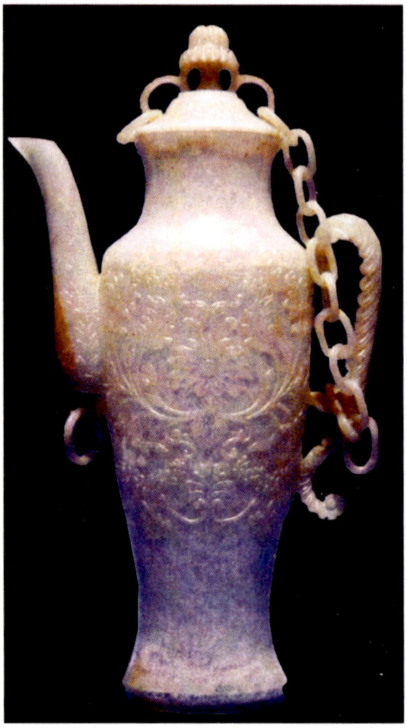

Pl. 34. White jade vase with a bud-shaped lid fitted with a chain and a spout, late eighteenth and nineteenth century CE

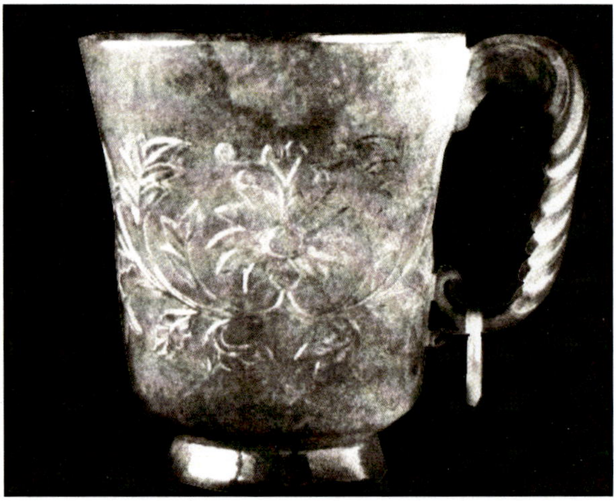

Pl. 35. A large cup or a bowl very thinly carved walls and floral motifs, nineteenth century CE